Now O' Clock
Being Mindful ... it Always is.

WILLIAM GARCIA

Book Cover Design by,
Octagon Lab.

Golden Hourglass,
Copyright: Dmytro Demianenko

Book Cover Collaboration by,
Garry F.Jeanniton

Copyright © 2016 William Garcia
All rights reserved.

ISBN: 0997516801
ISBN 13: 9780997516807
Library of Congress Control Number: 2016906434
Arttextry.com, Inc., Miami, FL

DEDICATION

I dedicate Now O'clock to my beloved late-wife Marilyn, our daughters Amada Mia and Bianca Jude and my son Angel Luis. It is also a very special dedication to my dear sister Dahlia for being there for the girls since their mother ran out of Life. Dahlia and my brother-in-law Pete filled a great void left in their little broken hearts, a void of silence now filled with an echo of love, care, concern, and affection. Living 2,000 miles away made it more important to Titi Dahlia and Uncle Pete to be there for the girls, and they were. I love them for that and wish them good health, happiness, and a long life together—they deserve it. I also dedicate Now O'clock to my brothers Jose and Junior, a big bro-man-hug for them; We're good.

Then there is Grandma, Tete, Malulu, Herman, and Patricia: thank you for the love and the care you gave so freely, and for being there.

To all of you I say, trust God, and as you do your best, be patient and trust your destiny.

CONTENTS

Introduction to the Second Edition	vii
Introduction	ix
A Mindful Cue	1
Life Lasts but an Instant	5
A New Conversation	9
The Joneses	12
Slow Down and challenge the Beast	15
One-Legged Man	26
Easygoing	29
TGIN	32
Retail Time, Measuring Now, and Seeing the Future	38
Numbers and Time or Energy Management	45
Only One or Two Seconds Longer; Children Do It	58
Instinct and Anxiety	69
Words Matter	72
Being, Then Doing	81
A Definition of Success, Good Fortune, and Goals Achieved That Never Arrived Too Late	84
S-U-C-C-E-S-S	89
We Can't Know, We Must Not Know, and Thank God It Is So	96
Her Last Best Friend and The Living Monument We Continue to Build for Her	102
How I Trust God, the Miracle of Luna, and the Blessing of Miracle	110
Training Wheels and a Lesson on Respect	128

Drunk with Choices	135
First Things First in the Present Positive Tense	138
Connoisseurs of Sensation and Emotion	146
All We'll Need	152
Life and Death	155
Doing	159
NOW	171

INTRODUCTION TO THE SECOND EDITION

Welcome to the new edition of Now O'clock. My intention in revising the book has been to expand on the different thoughts throughout and to include Mindfulness Meditation as a therapeutic holistic approach to better health and well "Being."

I discovered that the duration of Life, the speed at which we live, the wisdom in slowing down and "Being" mindful as a way to stay in the "Now" for just a few moments longer, involves fundamentals of Mindfulness. Included as well are insights into other aspects of Life as they to relate to Mindfulness.

As I learned more about the neurosciences and practice of Mindfulness, I became aware that, in essence, Now O'clock is about Mindfulness, and now that I have a better understanding, I would be remiss if I did not include my perspective as a Mindfulness practitioner relative to my thoughts about the essence and enigma of Time, and of Life and Living.

Now O'clock is not a book about neuroscience or the practice of Mindfulness Meditation. Nevertheless, I hope that I am successful in connecting Mindfulness as an added perspective throughout the book and making *Now O'clock* a more mindful and beneficial read for you.

INTRODUCTION

I hope that as you continue to read, you do not find me to be too repetitive because I will be reiterating ideas and being random at times as I shift from thought to thought. Treat my shifts in thoughts as an exercise in refocusing, fueled by your curiosity about the Thought itself. My restatements are based on my belief that some ideas merit repetition to get the attention they deserve. In politics, I have heard it said that if a lie is repeated often enough, it becomes believable, and this practice has been an effective campaign strategy. Here, I hope to create the same effect by repeating the Truth, as I see it, often enough throughout this book.

Just to qualify myself here, I am not a scientist, nor do I have a PhD in anything. Neither is the purpose of *Now O'clock*, to initiate intellectual discussions with those in the fields of neuroscience or psychology. Herein, you will find no in-depth scientific or psychological elucidations about what I write. I am a college dropout whose thoughts reflect empirical evidence of the past sixty years that I have lived "Being" in Time and having pondered thoughts I present here. I write for the curious mind in search of awareness, knowledge, understanding, and answers to questions I pose.

By the end of this book, you will see that I have developed a new awareness and relationship with Time and that now I have a fresh attitude and outlook about Life in Time. In other words, I am more mindful and in control now. Life is much less stressful. I am happier, healthier, and in peace in the constancy of Time.

I found that Time is not monogamous nor is it loyal to anyone. I know it is only here to spend my life away and that in the end it goes on without me as it has even before I was conceived. I also realized that we live our entire lives in the flash of an "instant" and that a Lifetime is not enough time to talk, to do, or even to write about my own entire Life; Time will just not allow. Therefore, my focus now is more on "Being" mindful and living life in the present positive tense rather than on keeping track of Time. As you know, we do a lot of that.

I also try to be as brief as I can in expressing my thinking and my meanings about love, family, success, aging, death, faith, and God.

In the first writing of *Now O'clock*, my editor remarked that I had a style of my own. I call it "plain English." She also remarked that I had written a good book, and I only hope that you agree after reading this revision. Again, and as you read on, I ask that you indulge me as I change subjects from time to time throughout the book. As said before, I may even be random at times. Please be patient and keep a present and open Mind.

In the end, I hope that at least one of my thoughts will inspire you to search for and find new meaning: new meaning you may be able to use in your daily life and that you too will have "Thought" occurrences that will move you to ponder and find meaning—meaning I hope you will share with at least one other person.

This is a short book so it will not take more than a *long moment* to read it from cover to cover. However, I am not suggesting that you speed-read through the book. I only ask that you "Be" in the moment and *Think* about what you are reading as you read. In "Being" so, you may also choose to be random in your selection of what chapter to read first and that's OK. I say this because some of the titles may get the best of your curiosity; if one does, go there. Irrespective of how you proceed, I believe there is something here for almost anyone.

What I write may help you change your Life as you *commit to being mindful and fully aware of the constant and present "living" moment.*

Being constantly distracted, our awareness of the passage of Time is usually treated as an afterthought. However, this is not to say that we should dwell on the passage of Time—of course not.

Instead, it is to "Be" aware that *Life and the passage of Time is one continuous and simultaneous occurrence so long as there is Life*. Metaphorically speaking, "*Life and Time are two parallel lines on a single page where stories of Life have endings but Time does not.*"

I realize there are practical reasons and applications for keeping track of Time. However, I hope to also inspire you to think and live in the full awareness of the present moment for only a few instances longer. I believe this will tune your sense of presence and awareness of "Being" as you are and as everything is in the Now, in the Instance of your life.

Taking Life for granted, I believe, is one of the undeniable Truths about "Being" alive. It is also one of those Truths too many of us live oblivious to. Perhaps it is a natural human tendency to take "Being" alive for granted; *all we have to do is breathe*. Even so, we do not have to appreciate "Air" as the essential giver of Life that it is. We do not even have to be aware that we are breathing; we do so involuntarily.

Here is a quick exercise: Right now, in this moment, pause and notice how you are breathing and then take a deep breath…I bet that felt good.

When again will you do this exercise and how will you be reminded to do it? Don't worry. You will have your own answer by the end of the book, maybe even before.

Unfortunately, we have become incessantly preoccupied with the activities of our daily and hurried lives as we try to keep up with Time. Our thoughts are usually about the future or the past. We are usually thinking about a Time in the future, (things to do) or a Time in the past (things we did), and I guess that is normal for us and the Times we live in. However, and in the meantime, "*Be" mindful and aware that the constant Instant (now) between the past and the future is the only Time we live and the only Time we can do something about almost anything.* I will remind you about this later on. Right now, I remind you to take another deep breath. That felt good, didn't it?

A MINDFUL CUE

Now my lungs are filled with a fresh breath of precious air, my mind is oxygenated and I'm ready to write about my first experience with Mindfulness Meditation. The experience opened my mind about my own "Being" and that of a special group of people. With them in mind, please indulge me for the next few pages.

I start with what I believe is one of just a few good definitions of Mindfulness. It means *"maintaining a moment-by-moment awareness of our thoughts, feelings, and bodily sensations as we pay attention to our thoughts and feelings without judging them, without believing, for instance, that there is a "right" or "wrong" way to think or feel in any given moment. When we practice Mindfulness, our thoughts tune into what we are, and surrounding environment. Mindfulness involves acceptance, meaning that sensing in the present rather than rehashing the past or imagining the future."*

Another definition is that *Mindfulness is an awareness of "Being" in the present moment as you are and as everything is without judgment.* In my mind, this is what I call *living in "Ism" as Ism is living in harmony with what it "is" and not what we wish "it" to "be."*

Mindfulness, for me, started when destiny introduced me to Gus Castellanos, MD, a retired neurologist, master Mindfulness teacher, mentor, and fellow practitioner. Feel free to Google him. As a military veteran, former law enforcement officer, and former first responder, I strongly advocate for the institution of Mindfulness Meditation training for those in these high stress occupations. My advocacy is informed by experience and studies that have been, and are currently underway with these groups, including correctional officers and firefighters, and the results are indeed encouraging. Gus has been involved in leading-edge Mindfulness research and is doing great work with these groups.

Empirical evidence shows an increase in mental agility, emotion regulation, attention, situational awareness, and better sleep. This kind of evidence presents an opportunity for the aforementioned organizations, which have instituted "Sensitivity" training as a means of understanding and improving relations with others perceived as different in terms of culture, ethnicity, or gender. However, these trainings do not focus on self-exploration as a means to actually understand and improve relations, and they should. Appropriately, evidence suggest that, used as a therapeutic technique, Mindfulness allows for self-exploration.

Lieutenant Richard Goerling of the Hillsboro Police Department in Oregon has instituted Mindfulness training, and they are experiencing positive results, not only in terms of the aforementioned evidence, but also in community police relations.

Furthermore, what concerns me just as much, is off duty and or out of service Time for those in the aforementioned occupations. These folks are like anyone else, except that they have chosen the dangerous profession of serving and protecting us all. Just the same, they have families, dreams and aspirations for a long, peaceful, healthy and happy life; a life empirical evidence show, is more attainable through Mindfulness.

As a member of the Board of Directors of the Dade County Police Benevolent Association (PBA), an association that goes above and beyond to protect the interest of its members, I would like to introduce Mindfulness. However, this I cannot do alone.

Until national awareness of Mindfulness Meditation makes its way at a local level, this is how you can help. Appeal to your local county government to lead the nation in providing Mindfulness training for those who serve and protect us. In view of the empirical evidence available, this is very important.

Meanwhile, there is something else I need your help with. It is something I have been spreading since I started practicing Mindfulness. It is about how fellow officers communicate with each other, specifically when we say, "Stay safe" or "Be safe."

For as long as I can remember, whenever I met an officer and was on my way, I would be told to "Stay safe" or "Be safe," and I would respond with the same words. These words are well intended and come from the heart; they mean a lot. However, when it comes to "words," I believe they matter. First of all, it is impossible to "stay" safe; nothing in life is static. Moreover, to "be" safe is temporary and situational at best and only to the extent that we have any control, and more often than not, we don't.

Today, after having learned and practiced Mindfulness Meditation for some years now, my caution has changed. Now, when I am told to be safe or to stay safe, I respond by saying "Be" alert; because it is what I want to be when I most need to "Be." The reality is that "Being" alert is a state of awareness necessary for being safe; otherwise, I am relying upon Luck, a chance I do not have to take. Being alert is "Being" in the moment, fully aware and mindful as I am and as everything is without judgment—that is how I want to "Be." The more alert I "am," the less I rely on Luck.

Rest assured, I am not suggesting that you always "Be" on alert for danger. No, that in itself is dangerous. Prolonged episodes under stress have been proven to be harmful to the "Self." Furthermore, it may even be worse than bad luck.

What I do believe, and what has been my experience, is that when danger is anticipated or is present, it's time to "Be" alert, it's time to be Mindful. "Being" alert is when I am best able to notice the subtle and the slightest change or movement whenever I'm in the presence of danger. At the same time, because my senses are keenest, I do not need to know that danger is present to be alert to its imminence.

So, the next time you run into your brother or sister, say, "Be" alert! Of course, I encourage friends, families, and all civilians to do the same for the few, the brave—those who serve and protect us all. So, please, I ask all of you to help me make the spoken words, "Be" alert, the Mindful cue to "Being" safe. Thank you.

Though I am partial to my brothers and sisters in the aforementioned fields, I strongly encourage everyone to take it upon themselves to seek out the knowledge and practice Mindfulness Meditation. After all, too many people, in one way or another and for too long, have been suffering from the effects of exposure to the insidious and stressful influences of the "Beast." Later in the book you will realize that you already know the "Beast" as a "what," not as a "who." The "who" is what "it" has conditioned us to become.

Thanks for your indulgence.

For those of you who have and are still serving and protecting us, THANK YOU.

LIFE LASTS BUT AN INSTANT

For reasons unbeknownst to me, I thought that I had first heard the words "*Life lasts but an Instant*" in the 1973 blockbuster movie *Enter the Dragon*, starring Bruce Lee. So, before I started to write this book, I wanted to be sure. I bought the DVD and watched the movie, at least twice. I was surprised and a little confused because nowhere in the movie were those words spoken. I had always remembered that the villain, Master Han, was the one who had uttered those words.

I recall the point in the movie when he had summoned co-star and martial artist Jim Kelly to his study. He wanted to find out if Kelly was a government infiltrator. You see, Master Han was the head of an opium production and distribution organization, a ruthless and paranoid man. In his questioning, he said to Jim Kelly: *We are born knowing only life*. It was at this point that I, for some reason, recalled him saying, *Life Lasts but an Instant*. If it were not for the action-packed series of fighting scenes that followed, I would have dwelled on those words for the rest of the movie.

Still, as I left the theatre that night, the words *Life Lasts but an Instant* seemed to be on a perpetual loop in my mind. I kept telling myself that the statement was dumb and foolish. It did not make any sense to me at all, but I could not get the thought out of mind. By the way, I also do not think the statement, *"We are born knowing only life"* makes any sense either, but that is a topic, perhaps, for another book. Still, I was not able to resist making mention of it as you will read.

For months after that night, the words *Life Lasts but an Instant* remained stained in my memory as I pondered the meaning. *It was said by a ruthless, but nonetheless, wise Shaolin monk. There had to have been a real and relevant philosophical meaning, but I could not figure it out.*

At the time, I was a dedicated martial arts student and practitioner, a brown belt in the Japanese martial arts style Nisei Guru Ryu. I learned in the old ways and Zen was an essential part of my training. I would meditate on the words *Life Lasts but an Instant* for months on end and, at some point, I do not recall when, it dawned on me, what I now believe those words mean; at least so long as I remember that Master Han had in fact spoken them.

Anyway, it was as if a light bulb turned *off* in my mind. *Eureka!* Yes, I meant to write "off." I believe that sometimes turning off your thinking about an idea allows new thoughts to occur and that was what I believe happened when I meditated. My first reaction to the revelation was how dumb and foolish I had been since the first time I heard those words. As in the 1972 TV series "Kung Fu," I guess you can say that, at the time, Master Han was the Shaolin monk and I was the little Grasshopper (student) played by the late-actor David Carradine.

I still do not recall when, where, or who uttered the words *Life Lasts but an Instant* even after I had watched the DVD a few more times. Perhaps the words and my recollection of it all is part of a dream I may have had or perhaps I, at the time, had slipped into a stream of consciousness that made those words prescient. Either way, the thought stands on its own merit and it was worth thinking, meditating, and writing about. Now I want to share my thoughts with you.

I start with what I believe is proof that Life does, in fact, last but an instant. Furthermore, what was amazing to me was that finding the proof was more about awareness than it was about research. In fact, the proof has always been there in plain sight and for everybody to see. Moreover, we, yes you and me, actually create proof all the time and so much so that the body of proof continues to increases by the second every day. Not only do we create proof all the time, we hint at it all the time with a phrase commonly used.

Do you know who first uttered the phrase, "A picture is worth a thousand words"? I didn't. Gum Gum, inventors of in-image advertising, didn't know either. So, they did a search and found that one of the earliest versions was in a 1911 newspaper article. It read, "Use a picture. It's worth a thousand words." Then, in 1913, a similar phrase, "One look is worth a thousand words" appeared in a newspaper advertisement. Some believe the modern use of the phrase may have come from an article in a December 8, 1921, advertising trade journal, which read, "One look is worth a thousand words," and later, on March 10, 1927, the phrase, "One picture is worth ten thousand words" appeared in an ad. Gum Gum concluded that the jury was still out regarding the original author of the phrase.

Regardless, when I first heard the phrase, it sounded like something a detective or lawyer would say.

Sometimes we look at something and see it differently from someone else looking at the same thing at the same time. Perhaps, this is the thinking behind the phrase, "Beauty is in the eye of the beholder." Actually, anything seen is in the eye of the beholder and, of course, that includes works of art and pictures. When we look at pictures, we see images of people, places, or things. These pictures usually bring back memories about the Time the images were captured, Time we can only reminisce about.

However, when the phrase, "a picture is worth a thousand words" came to mind, the distinction between seeing a Thing and thinking about the Thing suddenly occurred to me. It seemed to me that a picture could embody more than a thousand words, but what are those words?

The way I see it, a picture is the "Captor" of a precise Instant during the life of the person or persons in the photo. At the same time, it represents an entire Life filled with at least a million stories contained in an unfinished manuscript encompassing the total sum of knowledge and experiences lived up until that Instant. In other words, a picture will always represent one's entire life the instant the picture is taken. Therefore, if another picture is shot an instant later, it could not represent the same exact Life.

Who says the future has to be more than an instant later? It's still the Future. Who says that the past has to be more than an instant ago? It's still the Past. Just in case you are thinking it, I am not splitting hairs here. *I am though, splitting Life from Time as it elapses. In other words, I am splitting instances: the continuous and constant instant between Life and Death.* I hope you get the picture. How about we enter into evidence, a picture, perhaps even a "selfie," proving that indeed, *Life lasts but an Instant?*

By the way, if you have heard the words, *Life Lasts but an Instant* before now, please let me know where. Thank you.

A NEW CONVERSATION

We "are" because, as humans, we have "Thought," we think. Yet, at times I wonder if this ability to think is a blessing or a curse. It could be a curse, if we dwell upon a negative past or if we fear the future; Times that exist only in our minds. It can be an inspiration if we imagine a future with hope and positive expectations and remember our experiences in the past as lessons learned. *It can be an inspiration if we think of our future from the present positive tense.* After all, *just "Being" in the Present is in itself the ultimate Positive State.* It is a point in Time when the past, the present, and the future become the straight line we live on. This line is where there are three points that comprise our existence: point number one, we're born; point number two, we live; and point number three, we die—or, as I describe it in this book, we simply run out of Life.

Yes, like you, I learned and became accustomed to thinking about Time and Life as a cyclical occurrence. To me, this way of thinking is no different from thoughts about the Earth as being flat.

Life in "Time" is a straight line simply because there is **never** a precise repetition of any Thing or any Time. Time is an indefinite straight line through our lives and through nature. We age, nature ages, the planet ages, and that's just how it is. There is no old Time and there is no new Time. Enigmatically, *Time allows us the opportunity to experience a fresh sense of Presence in the Now. It allows us to always be new even as we grow old.*

There is no past Time or future Time; there is only the Present; the only Time when we can remember life experiences lived in a Time past and imagine life yet to be lived and which promise will only have value to those of us who awake in the morning. Still, keep in mind that *the idea of Tomorrow—and it is just an idea—is only a penciled-in promise of an imaginary Time to come. "Now" is as real as it gets.*

There is no "fast" Time and no "slow" Time. There are only our perceptions that Time flies, travels slow, or stands still.

Before I move on, I want to address a common misconception we hear all the time, "Perception is reality." This sounds good, but "reality" is in fact independent of "perception." They're not the same thing. Same and "very similar" are not the same things. Nevertheless, "perception" is real in whose mind it resides and may serve as a coping mechanism that allows one a way to deal with reality, its effects, and how we make sense of it. Because it is experiential, however, there is no right or wrong perception. There is just yours and there is mine. Perhaps you may find that our ability to have a meeting of the minds is best when we have very similar perceptions about a present reality.

Moving right along, as it was in the beginning and as it will be in the continuum, *there is only Time, there is only Now and the* **always** *becoming of the brand-new "You."*

Anyway, sometimes I wonder if this human ability to think is a trick played upon us by God or is it simply intelligent design? I do not know the answer or even if there is a definitive one that would satisfy everybody. Even if there was, I do not think it would make a difference.

From the Present, we can remember a Time in the past or imagine ourselves at a Time in the future. We can actually contemplate

Times when life does not exist from a Time when it does, the Present. Please do not simply dismiss this as obvious, be mindful of it. If it is impossible to have two thoughts at the same Time in our minds, and I believe it is, then we spend most of our lives ignoring the reality that we are "Being" in the Now. We are either thinking about what was or what is to be. Thinking about what "is" is not something we do a lot of and this lapse may be attributable to being constantly distracted and moving too fast. Think about it. *"Life lasts but an instant."* I believe I understand now, and with this new understanding, I have a more positive appreciation for Life with respect to Time, with respect to "Being" in the *Present Positive Tense*, and not just being alive, but mindfully living with hope, purpose, and passion.

There is a new conversation in my head about my life. It is about always being mindful of my own presence in the Now as I am and as everything and everyone "Is." After you read this book, you too will have your own new conversation.

THE JONESES

There was a time when most people did not know or care about who the Joneses were. That is perhaps because they were fictitious neighbors who had the best and the latest of what Modernity had to offer. As Time passed, more and more people heard about them, mostly through magazines, AM radio, and black and white TV. Many wanted to be like the Joneses and the trend "Keeping up with the Joneses" began. The media seized upon the trend, employing the most attractive Ads with powers of suggestion that could make you get out of bed in the middle of the night to go to the store to buy an advertised product or to do something. Usually, the "Thing" purchased was a "want" and not a "need," but it did not matter. What mattered was that, *The Joneses had "one" or the Joneses did "it."*

As a kid, I did not have a reason to know or not know who the Joneses were. Furthermore, I never heard my parents mention them either, much less try to keep up with them and we had AM radio, black and white TV, and magazines. Perhaps my parents didn't pay attention to the Ads. Anyway, we lived in a single-family home and did not need for much. I guess I can say we were

"Middle Class." Thinking back, I don't imagine our neighbors thought of us as fictitious.

I remember those times very well. It was during the late fifties and sixties when I was still a child. Everything seemed normal and Time cruised along quietly. It even seemed that people walked and talked at a slower pace.

In retrospect, I can see that it was just the way we lived. People had the Time and took the Time to care. When someone asked, "How are you?" a conversation about just how you were doing ensued.

Back then, nobody appeared rushed, especially on Sundays. Sundays were not considered "commercial" days, even though some "Mom and Pop" stores would open for a couple of hours. The only other place I recall being open was the church, and going to church on Sundays was just something we did religiously. There was no debating about whether to go because Sundays were believed to be for Family, thanksgiving, and especially Worship.

Unfortunately, those days are long past and once the Joneses had made their presence known to most, demand for products and services steadily increased. At first, local merchants stayed open a little longer just to be neighborly. Then, those same stores opened an hour or two longer to satisfy the extra demand. The surge in demand, fortunately or not, invited greed, and many participated. I cannot help but wonder if some business leaders and industry captains actually entertained the idea of lobbying the government to add another day to the week. However, even I can see how impractical and problematic that would be.

Today, businesses of every type are open on Sundays and many are now open twenty-four hours a day, seven days a week. I believe that 24/7 was the compromise to avoid adding one more day to the week; at least it seems that way to me. Perhaps another day added to the week would have been a better idea. What do you think? Of course, I'm being facetious.

Yes. I realize that today places of worship are still open on Sundays and that we have a choice to worship, spend the day with family, or go shopping at the malls. I guess if the Joneses can do it all in one day, so can you or I.

Today, keeping up with the Joneses is no longer the trend. We now live and behave as though Time travels faster than before, but this is only an illusion. The fact is that 24/7 is still 24/7, not an instant shorter or longer. We are now trying to keep up with the new fictitious space age family: The Jetsons. Accordingly, in these modern times, the ads are more attractive, instantaneous, and even virtual, making the power of suggestion that much more effective and insidious. Today, we are in a constant and shifting critical mass. Before you even learn how to use the latest electronic gadget, it becomes obsolete; there is a new latest version. But, that's how the Jetsons roll.

SLOW DOWN AND CHALLENGE THE BEAST

It is insane out there, but you already know this. I do not remember if I heard it said or if I read it on a poster somewhere: "Stop the world, I want to jump off." I can imagine many people still feel this way today. For some, the world is out of control and spinning too fast. Don't worry though, the person who flew by you going ninety miles an hour will be there at the next light. You know who I'm talking about. There was a time it might have been me—not this time though, I am here writing about that guy and about how not to be that guy.

Still, it does not stop there. I saw an Ad about some electronic service that said, "If you're not 50% faster, it's because you're 50% slower." Where does it stop, at 1000% faster? Well, recently and since the first edition, I saw another Ad that gave me the answer. It says, "Your tomorrow starts today," really! This is even faster that breaking the sound barrier. This is Life lived faster than the speed of Now, don't you think. Yes, I know and realize that it is impossible to live that fast and that the Ad is not meant to be taken literally. Still, these are market tested words designed to capture the imagination, and in an insidious way, they work.

Unfortunately, there appears to be no slowing down any time soon, if ever. Still, I hope so, but I do not think it will happen unless there is a definite shift in the national psyche.

Modernity can be unrelenting, as you can see. It is so much so, that we are fast approaching mindlessness at a time when we most need to be more mindful of our own "Presence," of our own "Being" in the "Now."

At some point, we have to become aware and take control because it's true. Today, we're constantly distracted and moving so fast we keep missing the Present. We need to slow down our pace so our Minds can see Reality for what it is and not what we wish it to be.

Check this out. The other day I ran into a friend of mine and said, "Hey, what's up, how are you doing"? He answered with the single default word we hear and use so often. You know the word: "Fine!" What's sad is that it's not an unusual greeting. There seem to be no Time for an old-fashioned chat, in person or even over the phone, since now the phone is used more and more for texting than talking.

Are we really so distracted and in a hurry, or is it that we're always running late? Either way, it appears as though we're living past each other. Now, why is that? I believe it's about being conditioned by Modernity or as I call it, The Beast. We had been distracted with chasing the tail of this beast, as it moved into the future with speeds that have since left the Joneses eating Silicon dust. The race to keep up with the latest advances in technology has us moving so much faster, and most of the time, for no good reason.

Here are two questions you may want to ask yourself and answer: Just how fast do I *want* to go? Just how fast do I *need* to go … to live?

As far as I know, the velocity of everything that is already fast continues to increase, and this could be a real sign that the Beast may never slow down. So, it is up to you to start.

Today, trying to keep up with the Beast is an increasingly fast-moving proposition. It's like trying to catch a greased pig. Just when you thought you caught it, it slips away and the chase continues. There is a new version of the latest tech device and you still have not learned all there is to know about the one you have.

Me? I choose to wait until the pig is a little older, slower, easier to catch, and cheaper to buy. Yes, I may not have the latest tech device, but the one I have does the job.

Still, it is not only about the speed of technology. The Beast, in other ways, has us addicted and distracted.

I am sure you have noticed that, over the years, businesses have been advertising the coming of all the major holidays earlier and earlier every year. Christmas, for example, comes to mind. Now, sadly, this is the norm and it is simply another frightening reminder of just how in control and insatiable the Beast is. Don't you get the sense that it's more about buying "Things" than about family and family Life, I do? If there was ever a Grinch, there you have it.

I dare say that we're addicted to the trappings of Modernity, and the addiction is so powerful that enrollment into consumer credit counseling "rehabs" is big business. Yes, as a nation, we need to rehabilitate ourselves because being conditioned as we are, we consume so much of everything there is and this can't be good. Make no mistake, *Modernity does not suggest Moderation.* Instead, its powerful influences suggest hyper-consumption and behavior modification. For example, nourishing ourselves is now more of a social event than a means of survival. Too often we eat just to eat and not because we're hungry but because it is "Time" to eat. You don't believe me? See if this is familiar. After a night sound asleep, we break fast when we wake in the morning. By the way, breaking an overnight fast is something we "do," not something we "eat." Anyway, then there is the snack before lunch, then lunch "Time", then the late-afternoon snack, the appetizer before dinner, then dinner "Time", and then there is dessert. Be honest here for a moment. Can you really be hungry the following day if what you are doing is eating just to eat, and not because you are following a dietary guideline; Obesity anyone?

It is just as bad when we buy even when we do not have a need for a "Thing." Then, when we buy the "Thing," we get a receipt (lure) that offers a huge discount if we buy another "Thing" by a date certain (the chase) after which the discount expires. I can imagine a fish being teased with bait and then hooked. We have become as insatiable as the Beast suggests we be. We have become "Thing-addicts." Junkies anyone?

Still talking about being hooked and addicted, the Beast already has legions of addicts, and like me, you're probably one of them. However, I believe the greatest number is among children and young people. They are easily hooked by lures, like electronic gadgets, video games that are as virtual as you can get, and social media, like Facebook, Snapchat, Instagram, and Twitter, just to name a few. The Beast keeps presenting new and more insidious lures that only disguise the effect of the addiction. It is the constant bait-and-shift that keeps us addicted so much so that disconnecting is virtually impossible. Of course, this only keeps us constantly distracted from "Being" human.

Here is a thought: *"Life is a continuous sharing of human emotions. It's OK to like things, just don't ever love them. It's OK to love one another, always do."*

Here is something else that I am almost sure you can relate to and that I should feel guilty about and don't: it's one of many other addictions to Modernity. If there is a rehab program for this kind of addiction, perhaps I should sign up.

Anyway, it's upwards of ninety degrees outside, I set the thermostat to seventy degrees and I get into bed and under a Comforter. Now, a Comforter is a quilt used as bed covering, but I use it to cover my body to keep warm. Mind you, I do this knowing that

I have absolute control of the temperature in my house and that I could otherwise set the thermostat to 75 degrees and cover myself with a sheet. I would be just as warm and save energy and money all at the same time. Spoiled brat anyone? Yes, me.

It all goes to show just how powerful the Beast can be and why reconsidering our relationships with Modern creature comforts, I believe, is a healthy idea.

Former President Bush once said that we are addicted to oil, and it is true. However, the whole truth is that we are addicted to almost everything that Modernity offers, and much of it requires the use of oil. If it seems that I am treading on Modernity, I am not. As you can see, I too enjoy creature comforts. However, what concerns me is the relationship we have with those comforts and how we become conditioned by powerful and insidious suggestions that trap us in those relationships.

I hear you, yes, breaking up is hard to do even when we know it's for the best. But, how do we break up with Modernity, we don't? We don't have to. It's more about control than it is about elimination. Besides, breaking up would take a lot of energy and time—energy and time better used to develop a Present sense of "Being" and being in control. It is, I believe, the best way to regulate the stressfulness of Modernity. It also helps to be able to slow down and hear ourselves breathe, to reflect on our own "Being," and to STOP, for a moment from Time to Time to be Mindful of our own presence in the Now. *Otherwise, we continue to behave as though there is no time for "Now," when "Now" is all the Time there is and all the Time we have.*

Here is another reason we need to control our preoccupation with Modernity and being modern. I believe we have all become just a little crazy, and in an abnormal way, "crazy" has become a coping mechanism that gives us an artificial sense of normalcy. *It makes me wonder if this "crazy" makes us see nightmares as ordinary dreams and reality only as vivid imaginations of our own present existence.* I wonder.

Still, Modernity can be a hungry and relentless beast. It chews us up and spits us out all the time, and we let it. We're stressed out in ways it seems we cannot escape because we are so addicted, distracted, too busy going nowhere in a hurry, trying to keep up, and at the end of the day, it feels like our bodies just "log off" instead of "shutting down." It's a small wonder we complain we're so exhausted.

It seems we're also conditioned to behave like drug addicts chasing the feel of the first High and *never* being able to capture it—it's crazy! Yet, I like to think we still have the option to *choose* not to chase the next greased pig, or are we helplessly addicted to Modernity? Which is it?

We came from Modernity as being a problem-solving proposition to one of *need* and *convenience*. Then, as Modernity advanced (as the Beast grew bigger, faster, and hungrier), we went from *convenience* and *choice* to *speed* and *choice*. *Speed* and *choice*, mixed with insidiously persuasive suggestions called Ads, has made the waters between *needs* and *wants* to become Brackish. The Beast is at home in these waters. "Come on in. The water is just fine," says the Beast. Unfortunately, because of the strong currents of speed, addiction, and distraction, we drift away from a calmer and more natural Life, a Life that is there for us to *choose*.

Instead, we live captive by the speed and control of Modernity and Connectivity. Seemingly all of a sudden, we are all wirelessly connected and constantly in touch with someone or something even when we don't want to be. But when we lose connection, panic sets in. Ever had your phone or computer broken, stolen, or lost? Then, you know what I am talking about.

We need to slow down, and I believe it would help if we would only disconnect more often and for longer periods of Time. However, simply disconnecting your devices is not helpful without turning off your *thinking* about them while they're off—otherwise, what's the point?

Here is a challenge that can yield benefits only you can experience and describe for yourself. There is no "one size fits all." However, it all fits in one Mind, an open Mind.

Start by disconnecting for three minutes a day during the workweek. Find where you can be alone and in a quiet place if that's available to you. Of course, you can do this with someone else, and I recommend that you do. Keep in mind, though, that those three minutes must be intentionally set aside. They can't be just a happenstance of free Time that somehow became available. The challenge is to be purposeful about the selection of the three minutes to do two specific things. The first, of course, is to be purposefully intent on disconnecting and the second is to be mindfully aware of that intention, being as you are and as everything is without judgment for the duration: just you, your breath, and your thoughts. Use this Time to notice your breathing and anything you may be feeling and sensing. This is the basis of Mindfulness Meditation, and unlike other teachings about meditation, 30 minutes is not required. However, if you find that you are not able to set aside three minutes a day at the office, then set aside 15 minutes during the weekend.

The idea here is to defy the Beast and take back control if only for three minutes a day, fifteen minutes on the weekends, or one day out of the year. Think of it as "escaping" from a reality manufactured by the Beast or weaning yourself from its milk (influence).

Just in case you're thinking about it, sleeping does not count as disconnecting. It has to be a Mindful and "intentional" disconnect. Over time and with regular practice, you will notice a calmer and less stressed "You." You will notice that it is easier to slow down and simply "Be."

Meanwhile, go for a stroll, preferably with someone else. Have an old-fashioned chat about how you're doing. Read a book, write, paint some art, or play a board game. Whatever you choose to do … just find your pace, your own pace.

By the way, there is already a national disconnect-day: it's called National Day of Unplugging. Join in!

How about this, I'm sure you've heard the phrase, "Hurry up and wait." Now it's "Hurry up and what are you waiting for?" A better question is; where are you going in such a hurry?

Here are a few other questions you may not have had to answer before. When was the last time you were not running late or in a hurry? Were you going to class, work, or were you going home after? Were you going to drop off the kids at school or daycare or pick them up? When last were you able to enjoy your lunch without care about what time it was?

I'm sure you can think of many more questions that could be asked. However, here is the ultimate question. It's the question I strongly urge you to be mindful about before you answer.

Is "Being" in a hurry or running late, something beyond your control? Barring events like traffic, inclement weather or an emergency, just to name the usual suspects, a sincere and introspective answer is likely to be an emphatic, No! In reality, we do have control. It's just that we allow ourselves to drift in the brackish waters of Modernity.

Keep in mind that when we try to keep up, only because the Beast suggests we do, we sacrifice the present living moment … *forever*. Unfortunately, too often we fall for it.

I hope by now we can agree that it's Time to slow down; that we should go slowly into that Midday.

Even so, I don't see this (slowing down) happening faster than the Beast would allow, having us under its influence. It keeps grabbing our attention with Ads calling us back again and again for the latest fix.

Who is in control here? If you agree that life is mostly about the choices we make, then we should *choose* to be in control. You decide how fast you *want* to go or how fast you *need* to go … to live.

You know that I enjoy modern creature comforts like anybody else, and I realize that slowing down may be easier said than done. But difficult is not necessarily impossible. You can slow down; the question is: Do you really want to?

Now slowing down will also require a shift in awareness with respect to how your life is changed from chasing the tail of the Beast; reflect on this.

As I said before, it's not about eliminating the Beast. That's not going to happen, nor is it necessary. I am talking about being mindful and in control as we *choose* how we want to live in the belly of the Beast.

Also, realize that whether we're trying to keep up or not, we will not be able to do all we *want* or *need* to do even if we lived a thousand years. There will *always* be things left undone.

Still ... tomorrow is not going to get here any sooner than it will. But this is not to say that we should not leave for tomorrow what we can do today. This sound like something the Beast would say. This kind of thinking is what has people saying there are not enough hours in a day to do all they need or want to do. *Come on, let's be real here. If you can't get it all done today, how are you going to get it all done tomorrow with the same amount of hours?*

Again, there are going to be things left undone regardless of how much you do or how long you live. Things like unread emails left in your inbox, for example. I'm sure you can think of others.

In the end, however, the reality is that we do not run out of *Time* ... we simply run out of *Life*.

Nike says, "Just do it." I'm telling you: "Just do it now ... *Live Now.*"

Unfortunately, there seems to be little effort to slow down and pay attention long enough to actually experience our own "Being" in the Now. Consequently, we keep missing the Present.

We should be mindful that *"Now" is that constant Instant between the past and the future and that it is the only Time we live and the only Time we can do something about almost anything.*

Now ... is always a good time to start *thinking* about taking control and slowing down.

These are times when we most need to be mindful of our own "Being" in the present as we *are* and as everything *is* without judgment.

We need to come back to "Being" present within ourselves and with each other in all the ways and for all the reasons that make us Human.

We need to be less preoccupied with Modernity and more mindful about "Being" in the Present; otherwise, we will continue to *miss* it.

Fortunately for me, I had heard about Dr. Jon Kabat-Zinn and his work on the practice of Mindfulness Meditation. His timeless classic *Full Catastrophe Living* inspired me. I started practicing regularly with a group led by Dr. Castellanos, and I'm here to tell you: I'm now less distracted, more mindful about "Being" in the present, more in control, and able to pace myself better. What would this be like for you? Think about it.

It's the result of taking Time out to be in a quiet place, to be still and alone: just you, your breath, and your thoughts. Of course, I encourage you to join a group as well, it's extra beneficial. Remember the three-minute challenge I posed earlier.

Now ... there is a fresh conversation in my head about my life and yours too. After all, we're all in this together. It's about always being mindful of our own presence in the Now—at least to the extent we are able to control speed, addictions, and distractions. But, of course, this comes with regular Mindfulness practice.

Still ... being mindful, slowing down, and being in control remains a challenge, because the distractions are many, the speeds continue to increase, and the influences are strong and deeply engrained in our psyche.

The Beast is no joke. It has a very tight grip on us. My hope is that by the time you're done reading, you will have already started *thinking* about loosening that grip.

Keep in mind that life is about people being here for one another and that Love, Compassion, Forgiveness, and Happiness are not devices of Modernity. These are attributes of our own natural *Humanness*.

We need to slow down to a pace where we can hear ourselves breathing calmly while *being* as we *are* and as everything *is*.

We need to slow down and pay attention to what *"Is"* about ourselves, those we love, and the world, and not what we would like or wish them to be.

So, here is what I encourage you to do: start a new day tomorrow, a new life, a Mindful life with a fresh perspective, and don't just to wake up and *smell* the coffee, but slow down and *taste* life one *sip* at a time.

ONE-LEGGED MAN

Our thoughts are usually about the future or the past and sometimes we are present-minded, talk about out-of-body experiences. As you can see, we have them all the time.

I remember a Time when people talked about Life as being a rat race in a world that seemed astronomical in size. Today, we have since left the Joneses eating Silicon dust and are now chasing the Jetsons in a world that seems so small. If one could afford it, and some can, you could set up a date, make reservations at a restaurant on the other side of the planet, and be seated and ready to eat in a matter of hours. We can get information about almost anything in seconds; all it takes is the touch of a finger. There is fast food, fast cars, fast access, instant coffee, instant messaging, instant this, that, and the other. *Consequently, in the fog of such haste, there seems to be no Time to slow down long enough to actually experience our "Being" in our own presence in the Now.* This gets more difficult as we become increasingly impatient with what is supposed to be "fast" or "instant".

I heard someone describe himself as being busier than a one-legged man in an ass-kicking contest. Now, just picture that in your mind and you can see how busy that is. At the same time, though, it is sad.

That same man one day decided he was going to disconnect and slow down. He was concerned with "burn out." So, he booked a flight to the beautiful island of St. John in the United States Virgin Islands. The tiny island is truly a getaway. It is tranquil, serene, and very private, a real tropical paradise. It was the perfect escape from the Jet race. However, amidst the beautiful sandy beaches, the balmy salt breeze, the waves kissing the white sandy shoreline, and the natural sound of Mother Nature singing, the man stretches out on a beach lounge chaise. He has a piña colada in one hand, a cell phone in the other, and a computer on his lap. It's easy to see what's wrong with this picture. It appears this man missed the point of his getaway. It was supposed to be about disconnecting, slowing down, and bathing in the presence of the experience. Nevertheless, this is his perception of what a getaway is. Fortunately, it doesn't have to be anyone else's.

Regardless of his perception, however, the reality is that he is actually in paradise, at least his body is. But off he goes, speeding on the information highway in cyberspace. He goes off on vacation but seemingly puts it on pause (yeah, right!) as he shifts his focus away from what is supposed to be his reason for being there. If you can't really get away, why bother? You don't go sightseeing while moving at 150 mph. You don't slow dance to fast music—you just don't.

Unfortunately, this man is not the exception; too often he is the rule. It is bad enough to be stressed and near burnout. But, to take your "Body" away on vacation and leave your Mind at the office is worse. Already, too many people behave the same way even when they're not on "Vacation." I say this to draw attention to the many who take work home during the week and also on the weekends. That's a lot of ruined evenings and weekends for children and families, and ultimately for the Self.

Could this be an addiction to a modern construct, the race to keep up with the Jetsons, the insatiable Beast, and with Time?

If that's the case, and I suggest it is, it's the pursuit of the impossible and a big waste of Life's energy. I remind you that even if we lived a thousand years, we still could not get it all done. Let me also remind you that you can be in control, you just have to take it. Start by asking yourself this question, "Is my life working for me and my family?" If your answer is a reflective and sincere Yes, then you're good. If your answer is a reflective and sincere No or not sure, then you need to get going. We are either in control or controlled.

I have always understood that we should pursue quality as opposed to quantity. Of course, if you can get both, great. Still, be mindful that any human activity can only increase at a decreasing rate. I learned this in an economics class in college and it is an important lesson because, in reality, it is a fact. Don't be confused, diminishing returns only applies to the Life, not to Time. *Time diminishes Life and there are never any returns.*

Perhaps you did not need to know this or believe it. Nevertheless, it is a fact about Life in Time. It proves the point I make when I say that Time spends us all into Nothingness or into "Something" we know nothing about. Of course, this includes all our physical, spiritual, and emotional experiences. Time was here before us and will continue indefinitely as we all run out of Life. Knowing this should be reason enough for anyone to retake control and shift their perspective about their own life. Try as often as you can to remind yourself to have your body and mind in the same place and time, to "Be" present in the "occasion" of your Life.

EASYGOING

Here is a story about how, in retrospect, I have always been an easygoing man. At the time I did not possess the "persona" awareness I have now. However, now I am also mindful about the great health benefits to be enjoyed by slowing down my life, especially in the *Jet race* we find ourselves in every day. We certainly can do without the G-Force (Go-Force) of Modernity that can be very stressful when we let it.

As you know, it wasn't until after I wrote the first version of *Now O'clock* that I started to practice Mindfulness Meditation. The more I learned and practiced, the more aware I was that I had always been mellow. Now I am even mellower and I attribute it to my regular practice of Mindfulness. Revising this book has also helped me to better understand and appreciate my way of "Being." I now feel relaxed in my life, happier and less anxious about Time. I know because writing requires me to plant my butt in this chair for hours at a time typing at the speed of Slow. Still, how fast I type is the least of my concerns and not my focus. It is a slower pace that allows me to relax, clear my mind, and focus on how best to share my thoughts with you.

Here is a little story I want to share. For some reason, being too relaxed appeared to have gotten me into trouble. It was a day in 1976, and I was ordered to report to the base commander's office and that usually meant big trouble. This was in Lack Land Air Force Base in San Antonio, Texas. I had to respond to a charge of doing or failing to do something. At this time, I really do not recall the nature of the charge. What I do recall was that I was known as and called "The Civilian" and maybe it was about that. Nevertheless, it had to be serious enough to require my appearance at the commander's office. I knocked on the door and heard a rough deep voice say, "Come in!" I stepped into the office, stood at attention, and saluted, "Airman Garcia reporting, sir," I said.

The commander had his back to me as he slowly swiveled around in his big black cushioned Command chair. He stared at me for a moment with his hands clasped and then asked, "Do you know what your problem is, Airman Garcia"?

I responded, "You are about to tell me, sir."

Oh! That seemed to anger him. "That is just what I mean, you seem to have a don't give a #@*! attitude," he said with an angry look. For a moment there, I thought he would jump out of his chair and get in my face.

Meanwhile, normally when you saluted, the command "at ease" followed—not this time, not with me. I had reported to the commander expecting at least a written reprimand. But, there was never a discussion about the reason I was standing in the Commander's office. Instead, I just stood at attention for the duration as he torpedoed expletives at me and then ordered me out of his office with a loud bark. I got the sense that the commander expected me to be nervous or scared or something, I don't know. Perhaps my easygoing demeanor and response to his question was not what he expected. It may also be that the "don't give a #@*!" attitude charge had nothing to do with the level of performance in my specialty. I was a Pediatric Medical

Service Specialist and I loved my job. Thinking about it, I suppose my commander was simply confounded or the charge, whatever it was, did not rise to a prescribed level that would warrant any form of discipline.

A few days passed and I never heard back from him or anyone else in the chain of command, and at the end of my tour of duty, I received an honorable discharge from the United States Air Force.

By the way, I was called "The Civilian" because it only appeared as though I had a regulation crew cut while on duty. Off duty, however, I was able to comb my hair out and blend in with the civilians. None of the guys in my barrack could do that, and hanging out off base on the weekends with a crew cut was not cool.

TGIN

So, what about this element we call Time, and what are you going to do with your Life while it is spent? Whether we realize or not, this is one of the most important questions we should answer sooner rather than later, I did. My answer was inspired by the awareness that while *"Being" is the Master key*, *"Doing" is ultimately the "unlocking" of the life I choose to live.* Being productive at a vocation or career and being there for someone else is a worthwhile use of Life. Positively affecting another person, be it your child, spouse, parent, friend, or a stranger, is a very good use of Life. Imagine if everyone made it a personal mission to positively affect just one other person, even a total stranger. Don't you think it would make the world a better place to live in, I do?

For now, though, forget Time itself. There is nothing we can do to stop it, slow it down, speed it up, extend it, or save it. Instead, we should focus on "Being" mindful in the present moment as we are and as everything *is* without judging. We should be mindful about what is important in our lives and the lives of those we love and care for.

What I mean here is that we should do for our loved ones those things that make a positive difference in their lives. Actually, doing anything positive for someone else or for ourselves makes a positive difference all around. It can be like spreading a contagious "Ease"; a positive act that does not have to be anything spectacular. It could be simply to say "I love you" or "I'm here for you if you need to talk." It could be the offer to bring someone a drink of water, a chair to sit on, or a pillow to lie on.

Especially with those we love, we can't know if we will have another opportunity to do any of these simple acts of Love. I say this because, *"Too many of us take Tomorrow for granted, not realizing there is no guarantee that the sun again will rise or that we may awake from sleep."* We can only hope, and when we do awake, why not love the person you're with? Here I use the word Love as a verb. I don't know any other form of the word. What I do know is that *there are so many more opportunities to Love somebody than there are excuses not to.*

Still, the act of Loving should not be limited to anyone in particular. You can love a relative, a friend, or even a stranger. The unfortunate thing is that there is so much distrust among people that if you were to attempt to commit an act of Love upon someone, he/she may get the wrong impression. You know what I am talking about. Now imagine if most recognized an act of Love and freely accepted it as it is, what a better world this would be. Remember that acts of Love need only be something as simple as a pat on the back with a compliment or opening a door. "Yeah, right!" Perhaps I am being naïve. But hey, I can hope. Will you hope with me?

Perhaps there is no way to get the message out to every human being and inspire them to love someone or even allow someone else to reciprocate, and again, I realize that I may just be dreaming here.

Still, I believe it is better to have a dream that never comes true than to not have a dream at all. Just imagine if every other person had the same dream. In a world that seems to exist more and more in cyberspace, a realm where being human is not applicable, it would make "Being" human the great awakening we all need on this side of Time. Now, imagine what that would be like.

Meanwhile, I will continue to love those around me every chance I get. My thoughts put in writing here are my act of love to you my dear friend, my dear stranger, my dear friend to be. Now it's your turn.

Here is a cliché: "We're all in this together." This cliché happens to be a reality of Life; it is true. We are all alive "in" the same Time. We are all alive, right here, right now and "Thank God it is Now" (TGIN).

It is also cliché to ask, "What's in it for me"? Herein lies the obstacle between the person and the act of Love, an obstacle dressed as an excuse. Well, let me tell you what's in it for you: It is the opportunity for you to act now, not later, not tomorrow. You do not exist then and so you cannot act then. You can only act here and now. To put off an act of Love for later may either be selfishness or carelessness and, too often, this may be attributable to being carried away by the powerful influences of Modernity, influences that keep us stressed out and busy trying to catch our breath.

Being in control and "Being" human makes it easier to be mindful about committing acts of love, even toward a stranger.

I realize it could be a bit uncomfortable and you may feel a little embarrassed to commit such an act, especially on a stranger. But, it is just Love, and because every one of us will eventually run out of Life, why not take the opportunity "Now" offers us and give a little more love or love someone you have not loved in a while?

Start with the ones you live with, then your friends and the ones you work with, or in any order you choose. Later, when you really get good at it, move on to strangers—one stranger at a time.

Listen, I realize that doing things for strangers may not come naturally to you and there may be good reasons for that. However,

I should remind you that your best friend, your first Love, or your spouse, was first a total and complete stranger to you at one time.

I also realize that sometimes we're just not in a good mood and that's OK. But, do you have to be in a good mood for someone to Love you? I don't think so.

Keep to heart that Love is more about "Doing" and *the feeling we have when someone loves us follows the very act of Love and when we reciprocate, there is Love for two. There is "Being" Loved.* What a good feeling, what a beautiful thing, this "Being" a Loving one.

By the way, this is not to say you must reciprocate with the same act. In other words, I give you a hug, you give me a kiss, you give me a hand, and I give you a shoulder to lean on. It's all about loving each other in our own unique way.

Here is a quote: *"We" make the world go around, not "I"; so add a little "Us" into your Life and thank God that "We" exist, together, right here, right Now."*

Here is another question I really want you to think about before you answer. Just how are you "Being"? I know, you're accustomed to being asked, "How are you doing"? Anyway, are you OK? I hope you are. However, let's just say, for argument's sake, that you are going through a bad experience. Would it matter to you what time or day it was?

I believe it is very important to not let the time or the days of the week determine how you are "Being." This self-determination should be based upon whatever is going on during your Life at a point in Time and how well you are coping. We live during and through whatever it is we're experiencing for however long it takes us to process, solve, and accept those experiences as we live onward.

Furthermore, realize that whatever it is you're going through, you're going through it in the Present. To hear this may seem obvious to you, but is it, really? Is it also obvious to you that there is no

Life an instant ago or an instant from now? Think about this for a second, really think about it. "Be" mindful that Life only exists in the "Now."

Try this. For just a moment, draw all your focus and attention to "Being" alive right here, right now. Start with noticing how you are breathing and then take a deep breath. Resist thinking about the past, however recent, or the future, however proximate. Now, is there something about which to be thankful? Of course there is; Life. Life Now.

Thank God, it is Now: *TGIN*. Try to live with an undying present gratitude for every breath you take. Be mindful of your "Being" in your own presence, wherever you are, wherever you go. Forget Fridays or Mondays. Forget about nine o'clock a.m. or five o'clock p.m. The clock or the calendar has nothing to do with boredom and fun, sadness and happiness, pain and pleasure, or love and hate. *It is all one Life, and there is only one "Time" and that time is "Now."* It's always Now O'clock when Life happens.

Remember to be mindful that you are always in the Present, always in the Now. Moreover, always be mindful that you have no choice, at least not in the physical sense because it is impossible to be in two places at the same Time, in the same Now. Only through thought can we transport ourselves into the future or into the past. Therefore, as we are in the Present and coping with whatever it is we are experiencing, we should try to be fully aware of "Being" as we are and as everything *is*, and think positively about outcomes in the future because it is whence those outcomes unfold. We should always strive to remain mindful in the Present Positive Tense for as long as we can. Yes, even if you are living through a negative experience in the moment, you should make an honest effort to think positive thoughts, beginning with the realization that the experience does not exist in the future and it is only as temporary as the Moment. Strive to be mindful of this as often and as long as you can. Also, keep in mind that just *being alive is the ultimate positive state on this side of the most powerful element that is: Time.*

I do not know who first spoke or wrote the words, "Every act of destruction is followed by an act of creation" or words to that effect. What I do believe is that in the formation of Life, there is no destruction. Instead, there is the most powerful and positive event in the entire universe and among all living creatures: Conception. Accordingly, *we are literally born Positive and it is from this Present Positive state, followed with positive thoughts, "doing" and positive expectations about the future, that a good Life becomes your Present and Mindful reality,* TGIN.

RETAIL TIME, MEASURING NOW, AND SEEING THE FUTURE

One of my other realized perceptions of Time draws a distinction between *"Wholesale"* Time *and "Retail"* Time. For most of my Life, I was blissfully unaware that I was a "retail" consumer of Time, because I had always been preoccupied with quantifying Time with watches, calendars, and other measuring instruments. Furthermore, I realized that keeping track of Time allowed me to wrap my mind around the numbers that tell me how much Time there is or what Time it is. However, there is nothing about Life and Being alive in this calculus, and I believe it is simply because Life exists only in the Moment and there is no way to calculate its precise measure.

You see, we live in increments of Time (Moments), increments I refer to as, *"Constant Instances,"* the reality of which is that *"Now"* is *the only Time, and all the Time there is, and as such, it is "Whole."* That being so, we should be always mindful that we live only in the Now, and that Now cannot and need not be measured as far as "Being" alive is concerned.

For how and when the retail use of Time conditioning may have come about, I use my birthday as one example. We all have a birthdate, right? For me, it is September 11, 1955, and when Time elapses to that date, it is tradition that I celebrate my Birthday. Personally, I don't see the sense in celebrating on 9/11 and it has nothing to do with the horrific terrorist attacks in the U.S. in 2001.

In reality, I was not born on September 11, 1955. That day is measured in terms of being 24 hours long, 1,440 minutes long, or 86,400 seconds long. It did not take 24 hours for me to be "born." In fact, I was born at a precise Moment in Time in the past, on a date we memorialized then as we do now as 9-11-55. To be precise, I do not have a Birth date; I have a Birth-Moment, a Birth-Now.

Personally, I do not celebrate 9/11, and if no one remembers, it would slide by unnoticed. In fact, those who remember seem to enjoy my birthday more than I do and that's OK with me.

Then, there is what I refer to as so-called ordinary days and they vastly outnumber the celebratory days. Therefore, more times than not, most of *the best days in any given year will* **not** *be one of the days we traditionally celebrate and it includes your so-called "Birthday."* For this reason, I rather think of 9-11-56 as the first of 59 anniversaries since my birth on 9-11-55 and nothing more.

As far as I know, it has always been tradition to celebrate "Birthdays." However, two things to keep in mind when thinking or talking about customary celebrations: Time does not repeat and because it does not, *it is impossible to be the same "You" twice. When you think about it, no one "Is," we are all continuously "Becoming" who we are to "Be" until a Time comes when we run out of Life.*

My "Birth-Now" occurred in an instant in Time and when I run out of Life (die), it will happen in an equal instant at a precise moment in the future. In other words, just as I was born some Now ago, so will I die some Now in a future Present. Furthermore, whether you realize it or not, *we will* **always** *live and die in the present, in the Now.* Of course, just as I was assigned a Birth date, so too will I be assigned a date of Death, a record-keeping detail—that's all it is. There will be an instant when my life is no more, as when

I was born and my life began. In fact, *when "Spermo" met "Eggly" in my mother's womb, conception occurred in an instant, and I've been living in constant instances ever since—so have you. I have always lived and continue to live "Now," so do you.*

Shifting gears again, I would like to talk about what I believe is another kind of Birth. When we were born, it was a physical birth. We were not born with knowledge. We had no "knowing" about "being" alive as Master Han would have you believe. However, we were born with the essential natural basic instincts necessary to thrive as we were cared for. Infants are able to react to sound, temperature, movement, and so forth. However, the infant's most important natural instinct is to suckle, thereby allowing it to be nourished so that it may survive and grow.

Infants also have a natural ability to learn as they are born as empty vessels to be filled over Time with knowledge, experience, and wisdom. As we grow, we develop a conscious Mind and every time we learn something new or awaken in the morning after being sound asleep, our conscious mind is expanded or "reborn". Does this make sense to you? I hope it does because *it is consistent with the inevitable and continuous "Becoming" of our "selves" with the passage of Time. It is consistent with the impossibility of being the same "You" twice.*

Getting back to "retail" Time ... here is a quote you may have heard and may live by, "Today is the first day of the rest of your life." Do you know it? Anyway, here again, Time is referenced in "retail" terms. I said it before: I cannot live one day at a time and I do not. Time with respect to Life is "whole" simply because Now is the only Time and all the Time there is. In reality, today is not the first day of the rest of your life. It is *"Now" that is the first "Time" of the continuous beginning of the rest of your life*. This is true simply because it is *always* the *first* Time you live in *this* present Moment.

If there is any doubt, here is an example to prove my point. Let's just say it is nine o'clock in the afternoon according to the most precisely calibrated Time measuring instrument available. From this precise point in Time, 9:01, or for that matter, 9:00:01 is a Time without life, without you, without me. It is a Time you've never, in your entire life, been alive before. By the way, I did intend to write the words "nine o" clock, in the afternoon" because it makes no difference. It is always Now O'clock and *we are always new or at least different, every Time, every Now.*

I want to get back to the numbers used to mark and measure Time. I found it easier to wrap my Mind around the concept of Time measured in retail terms than it was to wrap my Mind around the concept of Time as being "Now." The invention of numbers is what has made the concept of Time conceivable. Numbers allow us to manage our lives in terms of how much Time we need to do this or that, how long it will take to get there from here, how long we have lived, and so on and so forth. Numbers have made Life in a modern world practical and manageable.

Time is another matter in terms of how we measure "Now"—we don't, we don't have to. Besides, it is impossible to measure the present Moment. The closest I've seen "Now" measured is in sport events and in scientific tests. In sports, there was a time when the winner was determined to have won by a second or two. Now, that determination is measured in fractions of a second or microseconds. Moreover, in scientific tests, we can measure Time in terms of nanoseconds, which is one billionth of a second. This may be as close to an Instant as you can get. Now, try to wrap your Mind around this: *"Now" is even shorter and it is because our entire Life is cloaked in the "Now."*

Anyway, if we tried to measure "Now," we would always come up long. Because just the thought of measuring "Now" requires Time to elapse and that is before we even begin. In other words, in order to measure "Now," it takes Time and that Time will always be longer than Now. Furthermore, the use of Time is necessary in the absolute in order to form a thought or perform an act. Still, Time stops for no one or nothing. Therefore, as we tried to measure the Present Moment, we would have to continue to add to "Now," elapsed instances, while "Now" becomes "Then," which will have already elapsed and continue to elapse, never getting a precise measurement. At best we could only have a "Running" answer. Are you confused yet? I imagine you might be. In the end, we can only estimate or, better yet, not bother with the measurement of "Now" when it comes to "Being." Instead, we should just Live.

I guess you can say that each one of us *live in our own individual bubble of Time that eventually bursts when we run out of Life.*

Until then, consider that the saying, "He/she is in his/her, own world," merely references being suspended in thought, not Life. Here, I am talking about "Being" in Time as you are and as everything is without judgment.

Anyway, the subject of the Now is not something we ordinarily discuss, and I believe it is because it is too simple a concept for most people to appreciate. It is a subject usually left for Philosophers, Monks, and Meditation Gurus to ponder.

The simplicity of Life becomes complicated when we start school, are taught the one, two, three and the A, B, Cs so that we can learn formulas and concepts to solve and understand ourselves and Life's complexities. Still, this knowledge does not change the reality that there is no Life an instant ago, nor is there Life an instant from Now and that only because there is Life and intelligence do I read these words.

So, I leave the measuring of Time to those whose interest it is to do so. Meanwhile, I will just "Be," just live. *The fact is that nothing happens without Now. Nothing happens without Time and there is one and only one Time ... "Now."*

If it seems to you that I am oversimplifying the idea of Now, the fact is, I cannot. It just can't be done. The concept of the Present Moment with respect to our lives is as simple as it gets. In reality, I am actually amplifying the concept in "retail" terms. There is no other way to express the idea, and of course, it takes Time to do so. It could take more than a Lifetime and as long as this may sound, remember, *"Life lasts but an instant."*

I digress to say, that what I am about to write may cause you to think that I may be a little off—OK, a lot off—and maybe I am. I've talked about this with others and they thought I was being a little strange—OK, a lot strange. I hope to get a different reaction from you since this is the first time I put my thoughts about it on paper.

Ready? It occurred to me to ask myself this question: "Do I see into the future?" It sounds like a crazy question, I know, but stay with me. In terms of Time and Space, maybe I really do see into the future. Let me try to explain.

From where I am now sitting and writing, I can see the house next door through my window. It is the same Time in my house as it is there, at least so long as the house stays in sight and I stay in place. However, if I were to start moving toward the house it would be as Time elapses. I figure it would take about a minute or two to get from here to there. Knowing this, here is where it gets weird. Am I, in real Time, actually seeing into the future? Perhaps I am because as I move in Time and over Space toward the house and as Time continues to elapse, I am seeing the house as I approach it and until I get there.

In numerical terms, let's say that I started moving toward the house at 9:00 and got there at 9:02, that's two minutes' moving in Time and over Space while having the house in sight, while seeing the house as I approach it and then reach it.

It seems logical to me that the same applies when the weatherman says during inclement weather that visibility is one mile on the ground if you're driving or 10 miles if you're flying.

If this is so, is seeing into the future limited to people, places, and things within our sight and ability to get from here to there? I am not sure what to believe. I'm just asking. Perhaps there is a philosophical, mathematical, or scientific answer to the question, and so I defer to the experts. Still, what do you think?

NUMBERS AND TIME OR ENERGY MANAGEMENT

Wikipedia defines a number as a *mathematical object* used to count, measure, and label. The original examples are the natural numbers: 1, 2, 3, and so forth. A notational symbol that represents a number is called a numeral. In addition to their use in counting and measuring, numerals are often used as labels (as with telephone numbers), for ordering (as with serial numbers), and for codes (as with ISBNs). In common usage, the term *number* may refer to a symbol, a word, or a mathematical abstraction.

In ancient times, bones and other artifacts have been discovered with marks cut into them that many believe are *tally marks*. These *tally marks* may have been used for counting elapsed Time, such as numbers of days, lunar cycles, or keeping records of quantities, such as counts of animals.

Aryabhata developed the natural numbers 1 through 9 we use today in India around 500 AD. In the 800s, Persian mathematician Muhammad Ibn Musa al-Khwarizmi was among the first to establish the use of zero (0) to show powers of (10, 100, 1,000 etc.). Today, they are known as Hindu-Arabic numbers.

As it relates to Life and living today, numbers have many other uses. Modern uses are more sophisticated in terms of how we keep track of and understand nature and create order, sequence, and plans for the future. We also use numbers to manage our lives during the inevitable passage of Time. However, keeping track of Time and money seem to be one of the Beast's primary applications.

Still, numbers only give us the illusion that we are in control and my concern is about the focus we place on Time as it relates to "Being." If we agree that Life is a finite experience, we must also agree that Time is not. It is simply the way it is and it is what I call *"The Natural Equation" (TNE): L minus T, equals D. (L − T = D); Life minus Time equals Death (or Nothingness).* To complicate matters, we go about measuring Time with all sorts of instruments like watches, calendars, calculators, and gauges. The statements, "We are running out of Time," or "Time is up" ignore the fact that Time is infinite. *What we are actually "running out of" and "what is up"," is Life, pure and simple.* Time does not stop. It is why I continue to suggest that the focus should be on our energies, thoughts, and aspirations as we live and not so much on measuring or keeping track of Time.

TNE is the reason why as we are born, we simultaneously begin to run out of life (die).

Today, too many people still live in terms of days. I admit I too used to think in terms of living one day at a time. But I realized there may be countless moments in a day and I can only be alive one Moment at a time. Furthermore, being alive has nothing to do with what time of the day it is or what day it is. However, we have been taught and conditioned to focus more on Time and Numbers than on living Life.

Let's start with some numbers we are all familiar with: At age five, I start school. At 13, I am a teenager. At 18, I can vote. At 21, I can drink alcohol legally. "I live for the weekend." I am now 55 and can now get some senior citizen discounts. At 62, I can retire. At 65, I can collect social security. Sometime after I run out of Life, I die.

All these numbers show our preoccupation with marking Time even though we have absolutely no control of it. Granted, there are very practical reasons for tracking Time, the numbers we use to measure it and on planning.

Talking about planning, I know two people who lived their lives according to particular plans they had in mind and were successful at executing them. However, they were less than thrilled with how their lives unfolded at the end of their journey. I will call them Mr. Juan Massa and my Lady friend.

Theirs are stories about the use of Energy, Time, and Life. My Lady friend had a plan to work very hard, make as much money as she could, and save and invest until she turned 40. Then, she would retire and start living her life. Her number was 40. She worked her plan diligently, committedly, tirelessly, and almost obsessively. The idea that doing any one thing for 20 years as a means to achieve a specific goal and that it could consume you, had not crossed her mind.

It seemed to me that my Lady friend saw no difference between having "work" habits and having a "habit" of working. Working very hard for 20 years had become her lifestyle. Yes, 20 was one of her other numbers. Then the time had come when my Lady friend wanted some style in her life, but the only style she knew and had become accustomed to, was Work. She had put off countless Lifetimes for the promise of free time and money to spend in the future. Ironically, free time had become foreign to her. She now had to get used to it. She did some traveling. She visited family and friends, but at times, she worried that her visits were more of an inconvenience to those she would visit. It did not matter that they were friends and family. You see, her family and friends did not plan their lives as she did. Most of them lived a modest life, and from paycheck to paycheck. They were just as busy with their daily and hurried lives. Free time to them mostly amounted to days off, weekends, and holidays.

At some point, my Lady friend realized two things: she was still relatively young and it would not take her another 20 years to do all the things she wanted to do. So, she went back to what she knew and had become very accustomed to: her habit of working.

Mr. Juan Massa's story was similar yet different. When I first met him, I was a civil deputy sheriff with the Miami Dade Police Department. My duty was to locate people to serve them with legal process. So, from Time to Time, over a period of about 10 years, I would stop at his place for a shot of Cuban coffee and we became acquainted. He was a very likeable and hardworking man and because I never knew his name, I refer to him as Juan Massa, which is Spanish for John Doe. Anyway, he always treated me as a special customer. In fact, he treated all his customers with a special care and concern. At the time, he may have been about 55 years old, even though he looked much older. He looked like "Hard Work." Not too long after, I was reassigned to a different work zone and did not go back there for coffee again.

One day, I had to locate a person living in a luxurious high-rise condominium penthouse. I rang the doorbell and it was the owner of the coffee shop, Mr. Massa.

We instantly recognized each other. He greeted me with a bear hug and invited me in. It had been a few years since I last saw him. The apartment was fabulous. It was pure luxury, marbled floors, chandeliers, leather and mahogany furniture, and a 180-degree ocean view that caressed the eyes. It was like a dream or something out of a magazine. I turned my attention back to him and noticed the obvious. Time and hard work had sculpted him into what looked like hard work done long and wrong. He had aged very much and he moved slowly and warily, as though in pain. I could see it in his face.

Either he knew the purpose of my visit or it didn't matter. Nevertheless, it mattered to him to have me sit down for a little old-fashioned chat. He said to me, "Look at me. I am rich and now live in the lap of luxury. I worked very hard most of my life to get to where I am today. But the long and hard hours, days, months, and years of work now sit on my lap. I struggle to get up once I sit down. I take all kind of medications for this, that, and the other. Often, when I leave my luxurious home, it is to visit my doctor. My wife is in bed and she is no better off than I am. She has always been my right hand. Now she is just right there, sick in bed."

I question those who say that hard work never killed anyone. Ask my Lady friend and Juan Massa just how they feel about it. Obviously, hard work did not kill them in the physical sense. The 20 years trapped my Lady friend between work habits and a habit of working. Juan Massa and his wife were physically distressed and spiritually fatigued.

Now, don't get me wrong. I am not against planning for a better life. In fact, we should. Neither am I against hard work in order to realize whatever you believe the American dream to be. I encourage Success in the pursuit of goals. What I am against, however, is *all hard work and little or no play today.*

I strongly encourage you to have dreams and plans for getting from here to there. However, I encourage you to do so being mindful that the essential ingredient is Time, something we have no control over. Your plans and dreams are not a Present reality. They exist only in your mind as Thoughts. Being here and now and working on your plan is what you should be doing if you are to increase the chances that your dream will come true. However, *"To make dreams come true, one must first wake up, get out of bed, and take action."* Also, keep in mind that you are living your "entire" life now, and that your plan for success is but a fragment of your life.

"You have a long life ahead of you." I'm almost sure you have heard or read this quote before. However, the quote references a

Time that only exists in the Mind. Meanwhile, I am here and now and have a lot of living to do and, as you already are aware, all that living can only be done in the Now. Still, we should be mindful as we try our best to balance working on our plans and enjoying the present living moments we have. Of course, trying to control anxieties and impatience about your future will be challenging, but we must not sacrifice our own presence in the Now. We must be patient and confident that *soon enough our dream will be our present "Living" reality.*

At the beginning of this chapter, I mentioned the use of numbers to *manage* our lives during the inevitable passage of time.

The Encarta English dictionary defines Management as, the organizing, directing, handling, or controlling of. The same dictionary defines Time as a period or moment.

Accordingly, and being consistent with my thoughts about Life in Time, Time "management" is not an idea I should take literally. But for many years, I behaved like I could and it drove me crazy. I later realized that what actually drove me insane was the marriage between Numbers and Letters; Numbers used to mark Time and Letters combined to create words used to name, Months, Days and certain stages in our lives. I'll explain in a moment. Anyway, I've come to see the concept of Time "management" as nothing more than an illusion; it cannot be done. It is simply impossible. The best I can say about it is that it may just be a practiced mental exercise. More importantly, though, we should be aware and mindful that it is just that.

Before Numbers (BN), the concern may have been the duration of daylight and what and how much could be done in order to survive. It may have also been about how much darkness there was before there was light again. BN, it was always Now O'clock and man was only as old as he/she was able to "Do" in order to survive.

So, I can see now that, in reality, it is numbers in a 24/7 world that drove me crazy. Now there is a "Time" for everything and a corresponding number to mark the stages we live through. I gave this example before, but here I expound. At 13, we are teenagers; at 16, we can legally drive; at 18, we can vote; at 21, we can drink alcohol legally. By this time, we are building a career and a Life. It is time to study/work long hours, usually hurriedly and running late, hectic days, drawn out months and years, chasing goals and dollars while we're still "young."

I was that young man about 20 years old and being told by a Judge I worked with, that if I hadn't achieved my goals by the time I was 40, I should *forget it*. What made 40 a defining number with respect to achieving my goal was something I could not subscribe to. Life continued to happen and I forgot that I was no longer 40. In fact, when I turned 40, my brother asked me about "Gray Balloons." I still don't know what that was all about.

Anyway, later in life many begin to do what only aging folks do: defy numbers saying things like, "age is just a number" and "it is not how old you are but how young you feel" and "I do not look my age" and on and on. As "seniors," we find ourselves on the descent of our mountain of Life with our health care belts fastened, the preoccupation du jour, and with feet heavy on brakes that don't work. The reality of being a certain age affects us and Time "management" is ejected. Most of us call this "retirement age" and this to have a corresponding number somewhere between 62 and 67.

It is a time when our mortality has center stage and when we start doing what we should have been doing all along: managing our energy, something we always had control over but relinquished it to our preoccupation with Numbers (Time "management").

Now don't get me wrong, numbers have utility in our lives and in some cases they save lives. For example, it is one thing to say that hurricane "Wind Blow" will make landfall soon, as opposed to saying that it will land in 72 hours or taking prescription medication every four hours for maximum efficacy.

Since I started writing Now O'clock, Numerical Time got my attention and my focus shifted. It became less about Numerical Time and more on the supply of Life Energy I have. This doesn't mean that I now disregard numbers; they will always be useful. I still get things done by a Time they should be or need to be done. The difference is that now, more than before, I am mindful about my energy.

I may always know how much Time there is. I will not always know how much energy I have left, much less when I will run out of Life. This is why I am not so concerned with stepping on the brake of Life as a way to defy Numerical Time.

Here is something else about Numerical time that I find enigmatic: As I was writing, it occurred to me that different states and countries have different "Time zones." It should be apparent to you that this goes against everything I have written about so far. For those who wonder about the different "Time zones," think about this for a second. During the summer months, the assigned Time difference between, let's say, Miami and Arizona is three hours. When it is three o'clock p.m. in Miami, it is twelve o'clock p.m. in Arizona. However, the reality is that there is no Time difference when it comes to "Being" alive. There are only numerical differences used to express Time, the same numbers invented by man; numbers better used for Activity Management. *Yes. I said Activity Management*, not Time "management." Remember, it is impossible to "manage" Time.

I've said it before and I say it again: We can't stop it, start it, pause it, rewind it, or fast-forward it, or save it. Time just *is* and will always be. As far as "Being" alive, the top of the planet and the bottom of the planet are the same age. The fact remains there is only one Time and that Time is "Now." This is true for everyone and everything on planet Earth. Everywhere you go, no matter the number used to express change in "Time zone," it is always Now O'clock. Similarly, it is true that if a tree falls in any forest anywhere on the planet and there is no one there to hear it—yes, it stills makes that crashing sound.

Think about this for a moment. As I am writing now, it is 10 o'clock p.m. in the east. It is seven o'clock p.m. in the west. There are "three hours" differences between "Time zones." The phone rings and friends out west announce the birth of their first child. Now, think about this before you answer: What time was the telephone connection made; the time you first heard the voice on the other end of the line—ten or seven? Well ... here there is only one correct answer. It is impossible for any single live event to occur at two different Times. Now, let's beat the dead horse and ask a second question. Was the child born three hours in the past or, vice versa, three hours into the future? Neither, right? However, and just for record keeping purposes, the child was born at seven o' clock. Still, just as Now is the only Time we can be alive, Now is the only Time we can die and so the child was nevertheless, born Now O'clock.

Here is another example. Right now, it is 11:05 p.m. here in Miami and 12:05 p.m. in Japan, a 13-hour difference. If I were in Japan and boarded a flight to Miami, would I be traveling 13 hours into the future? Of course, not. Remember, there is no future or past with respect to "Being." *Life and Time travel together anywhere and everywhere, but only until we run out of Life.* Again, Time does not begin nor does it end. Time just is.

In life, we first appear, live for some time, and then we literally disappear into the dustbin of the past. Time makes sure of it. Oh! By the way, here is another question you may have heard asked before. If numbers were never invented, how old would you be? You couldn't know. There would be no language to express age. But thanks/no thanks to letters and numbers, we can.

I digress. From the moment we are born, our life energy source increased but at a decreasing rate. Time, on the other hand, remains a constant that is always beyond our control.

Here is an example of Energy Management. While they were in high school, I would tell my children that when it comes to homework, they should start with the most difficult task to the easiest. You see, by the end of the school or work day, our physical and/or mental energy is lower and we are weaker and/or tired. Concentrating is difficult and staying awake becomes impossible.

The same may be true about working out. Now, I am not a workout guru, but it seems to me that if I were to follow a workout regimen, I would need to have the energy necessary to complete the regimen. Perhaps there could be a regimen where the goal requires most of your energy be used at the beginning. In either case, Energy Management is most useful.

Let me say something about working out. I cannot and will not deny its benefits. However, I can say that often enough, I'm not motivated to work out. I just don't feel like it. But when I do, I am always glad I did. I said this to a friend and he said that whenever he felt the urge to workout, that he would lay down on his sofa until the urge passed. Of course he was joking.

But why would we want to do the impossible ("manage" Time)? It does not matter what you have to do or want to do by a certain Time. Try to be mindful that Time "is" irrespective of Life and that your Life is a finite experience; much less is the amount of energy you may be enjoying at the time. It matters not to Time how much energy you have or don't have. It does not slow down so you can get things done by a particular numerical Time. Stress anyone? Time is always a constant and inexhaustible element and Life, as is energy, is a diminishing and finite one.

Have you ever heard a meteorologist talk about "Weather management"? If you did, you would think the meteorologist was crazy, wouldn't you? Of course you would. Well, we can no more "manage" Time than we can "manage" the weather.

Trying to do the impossible is a futile and a self-inflicted stress we endure even knowing we don't have to. Listen, we were born in Time and when we die, it will simply be because we ran out of Life, not Time. Remember, Time is irrespective of life. However, there can be no Life without Time. This is why I say: Forget Time "management." Instead, I believe we should shift our focus toward managing our diminishing and finite supply of energy and use it according to what activities have priority—this we can do. On the other hand, we can do none of what the dictionary says about Management with respect to Time. Time just is, and it elapses as it does and there is no way to stop, pause, rewind, or fast forward it. There is just no organizing, directing, handling, or controlling Time.

By the way, here is something I find peculiar. I know people who set their clocks and watches anywhere from five to 30 minutes ahead and I am almost sure you do too. One of those people may even be in your mirror. Anyway, I was told that it is a way to help them be on time or give them some extra Time to be on time. This apparently works for them and, I guess, that is all that matters. To each, his own Mind.

Anyway, this behavior may sound like Time "management," but of course, it can't be. Ruling that out, then what is it? It seems to me to be some sort of manipulation, but manipulating what? This was explained to me by a friend and my understanding was that he was always aware of the real numerical Time. Still, setting his clock or watch gave him a sense of control in terms of Time and his ability to get to and from on time, so that he felt less anxious. If he needed to be at the office or at an appointment at 3:00 p.m., he would likely get there on time and not necessarily five to 30 minutes early, so why the manipulation?

To me, having two different Times on my mind as it relates to a single event (meeting) seems more stressful than "Being" in real Time and arriving at the event in real Time; when it is 2:00 p.m. in real Time and my clock or watch shows 2:00 p.m. In other words, it being 2:00 p.m. in real Time, while my clock or watch shows 2:05 or 2:30, seems to require the mindful suspension of one Time or the other. Yet, by all accounts, we're usually on time in real Time, so why the manipulation in the first place? Why play tricks on my own mind? Then again, to each his own Mind.

I suspect the Beast has something to do with this kind of behavior. It already has us conditioned in so many ways and I can see its influence at work here.

Meanwhile for me, there is something about real Time and the awareness of my Presence in it. It is the only Time I can be mindful about managing my energies and prioritizing my activities.

I realize there are practical reasons to keep track of Time with respect to what we need to do to live. But, here is where the operative word "Do" applies. We talk about "spending" Time, when in reality, it is Time that spends us all into Nothingness or into "Something" we know nothing about. We commonly refer to this expenditure as Death.

Yes, it's good to know the time of the day, month, or year. But, having such knowledge is of no use to us without first "Being" and then "Doing" something with our lives. Tomorrow is likely going to be here whether we "Do" or not "Do." What we don't do today leaves us one day less to do it, and that's one day less forever.

Each one of us is in the lottery of Life and we cannot withdraw until our Life is played out. Therefore, we should be doing what we need or want to do as often and as best we can. Of course, there will be Times when we may need to prioritize. However, when we do, we should determine if a priority could be based on Energy as opposed to Time or both.

Here is where management works toward outcomes. None of us has limitless energy and none of us knows how much life we have left to live. Time is a perpetual constant, period. Energy on the other hand, is not. However, there are things we can do to preserve energy. Obviously, we need energy to be able to do what we need to or want to do to make it through the day, to enjoy Life. If we already have the energy we need, then it is only a matter of managing it, using it at varying degrees, retaining and replenishing through rest, exercise, and nutrition. If you do not have the energy you would like or need to have, then it is a matter of starting an energy plan and/or a workout regimen. Of course, if your lack of energy is due to a real physical inability, then a modified regimen could be followed in a manner that does not result in worsening your inability, but enhances your energy level moderately or within acceptable levels. I recommend the advice and guidance of a nutritionist and a fitness trainer. Even for those who are now enjoying the highest energy level ever, there will always be limitations attributable to that which is impossible to manage: Time.

Of course, there is what I believe to be the most important use of energy and that is mental energy—the burning of brain cells, so to speak. My daughters manage their mental energy when doing homework by tackling the more difficult homework and or homework that is due first, leaving the easier ones for later. Imagine leaving the hard work for later in the night when your eye lids are heavy, your mind is fatigued and the clock continues to tick. The quality and accuracy of your work will show.

Humans are not machines and even machines need downtime in order to manage wear and tear. Like humans, machines have a life span. The difference is that we can pretty much calculate the end time of a machine's usability. Humans on the other hand can run out of Life at any moment, regardless of age or health. In the meantime, try to be mindful that your Life Energy can only increase at a decreasing rate and that this basic economic postulate does not apply to Time.

ONLY ONE OR TWO SECONDS LONGER; CHILDREN DO IT

More than ever before, we are now able to wrap our minds around complex theories and concepts. However, it appears that all this brainpower and the strong, and too often insidious influences of Modernity, have made it easier to take the simple reality of "Now" for granted, even knowing that "Now" is the only Time we can do something about almost anything. I can hear you thinking, "This man is being redundant about the obvious. I know that 'Now' is the only Time anything can be done." Wait a minute here. I am not suggesting you do not know or realize this. I am suggesting, however, that simply because it is obvious, we seem to take the Present for granted and that Modernity plays a controlling role. The concept of "Now" is the kind of knowledge we keep stored in our subconscious Mind as we scurry around trying to keep up with the "Jetsons." *I am also suggesting that "Now" is just as obvious and just as redundant simply because it is always "Now." It is something we can always count on so long as we're alive.*

One of my goals in writing this book is to suggest and encourage you to *revisit the concept of Life in Time and in the perfect Present, which is "Now."* I encourage you to *make a conscious effort to try to stay in the Present Positive Tense, if even for only one or two seconds longer, from Time to Time.*

This is not as easy as it sounds, yet it is simple. Even so, it requires a commitment to take the Time to pay attention to the fullness of your own mindful "Being" in your own presence, your own "Now" as often as you can. Here again, I am talking about Mindfulness. This practice has made a difference in my Life and I'm now better able to "Be" in harmony with Life in Time as I am and as everything is without judgment. This helps with my volitional ability to perceptively slow down a couple of seconds so that I am better able to set my own pace, physically and mentally.

Living in harmony has changed my life and it can change yours as well. I now have a fresh perspective about Time and Slowing Down, even knowing that Time itself is a perpetual Constant. Here, my focus is on slowing down the Mind with the intent to control my sometimes frantic "Thought surfing". However, physically slowing down by walking at a slower pace or driving fewer miles per hour (mph) can also help. Doing this has made a difference in my daily life in terms of "Being" and in how I now perceive Time. To maintain my adapted perception of Time, I get the tune-up I need through the regular practice of Mindfulness Meditation.

Here is something to which I'm sure you can relate and how regular tune-ups can help. The experience of what I am about write is similar whether it's traveling from home to work or from work to home. I focus on the trip home from work. For me and for now, it's more about family than it is about work or business associates.

Have you ever sped up to pass another car on the highway because you were in a hurry or running late? I bet you have. Before I continue, I'll be the first to admit that I was a habitual "speed" offender who has since been self-rehabilitated.

Anyway, when I sped, it felt like I had made great progress toward getting to my destination—of course, I did. However, I do not recall what metric I used, if any, to measure what progress I had made, but it didn't matter. I had advanced at least beyond the car in front of me and now had less distance to travel. Time was less of a factor than was Space, even though I had not considered any distinction between the two. However, the amount of Time elapsed was only an illusion until I realized that I had only advanced a second or two.

Looking back, was I crazy or out of control? Of course, I was not crazy, unwittingly though, I was trying, uncontrollably, to keep up with the Jet race of Modernity and behaving as if I could live faster than the speed of Now. I was addicted to Speeding on what I call the Treadmill of "Now." What insanity, just to arrive at my destination two or three minutes earlier.

Obviously, up until that Time, I had been lucky, and so were fellow road travelers. It was a stupid risk I took without giving it a second thought.

I recall the anxiety and the stress of being in a hurry and going for the Pass while trying to avoid a crash and knowing I could kill myself or someone else had I made a mistake. However, now that I am able to give the situation a second thought, I realize just how crazy it was because I was not the only one taking the same foolish and dangerous risk.

Then there is the person who is just cruising, perhaps between the two crazies. He's not looking for a crash, and like me, he just wants to safely get home to his family. Unlike me, it may be that he was just driving Mindfully.

So, for me, being in control was at best a 50/50 proposition, maybe less, much less. Being lucky on the other hand would have depended on the size of the rabbit foot I might have had in my pocket, and I didn't have one.

Anyway, the anxiety, the stress, the High of speeding was no different from being under the influence of a mind-altering drug. So out of control I was that by the time I got home, I was very exhausted. It is no small wonder that, at the end of the day, I had little enthusiasm and energy left to actually enjoy my evening. The time with my family only seemed to add to the stress, and it was because my emotional tank was near empty, and my children, with their tanks full, were always there waiting to greet me. I was not at my best for them. I knew why, and it bothered me. I had to make up my mind to take control and I did so through regular Mindfulness tune-ups.

Listen, Life is one great journey paved with many short trips, and driving home is one of those trips, the kind of trip best made while Mindfully tuned.

Now, I practice Mindful driving and when I find myself among the crazies and I feel the onset of stress and the urge to speed, the first thing I do is turn off the radio or CD and all of a sudden, I am in a different world. My Mind begins to slow down with the abrupt silence. I notice my breathing and I take a deep breath. I am now feeling so much better, more relaxed, and I can actually feel "Being" in my own presence in this new Mindful, silent, and safer world. I start to notice my grip on the steering wheel loosening. The muscles in my back, shoulders, neck, legs, and feet start relaxing. I notice the car in front of me and the one in the rearview mirror and the others driving by. I am breathing calmly and I am now fully aware of what I am doing and what is going on around me. "Oh! There goes a crazy one, and another!" I nod my head almost in disgrace remembering that I was one of the crazies. I come back to "Being" present and I now notice the weather and the scenery. I've driven by here many times and I never noticed this or that or how beautiful it all was. It is one thing to get a glance or not see at all, but to slow down mentally and physically, I get to notice more about what I am doing and about everything else and my life is safer and better for it. The crazies on the road are in luck and are safer now that there is one less crazy on the road as I settle in and turn on the Cruise control of my Mind. At this point, I can turn my radio or CD back on, and when I do, I reset the volume much lower than it was before I turned it off and the sound is still loud and clear. Then, again, most of the time I stay in my silent and Mindful world until I get home. I'm good.

It was no longer what time I got home. It was now, how I got home, and when I did, I was ready for the "rush" that awaited me. My emotional tank still may not have been full, but there was enough enthusiasm gas to enjoy the evening with my family.

It was a while after I started regular Mindfulness tune-ups that it occurred to me that I had never checked my arrival time at home. However, what I can say with absolute certainty is that it was exactly the same time then, as it is now, Now O'clock—being Mindful ... it always is.

When I think about it, I realize that the whole concept of Mindfulness is not new to us. It is something we lost even though we did not have the mental capacity to know we had it. We were indifferent about Time. However, we instinctively knew that it was "Now" O'clock. Of course, this was before we learned about numbers.

Anyway, as children we did not need anyone to tell us about "Being" and staying in the "Now." It came naturally to us; at least it seemed that way. You see, as children we had very little experience with Life or Time, so our memory banks were not as full and as stained as an adult's was. Our thoughts about the future were just as limited. For our parents and adults in general, Time seemed to fly. For us, Time seemed to stand still, the future seemed too far away, and trying to think about it seemed useless because we had little or no reference. We lacked the Life in Time experiences that would allow us the ability to formulate clear imaginations about a future Time. Ours was a smaller world.

Thoughts of a future are a developing concept for very young children, and of course, that development came with time and experience. This is why I believe as children, we spent most of our time absorbed in what we were doing, in the moment (Now); it was all that mattered. At play, we had a natural ability to block everything out because *being mindfully present was Timely and Natural to us.*

This is something we lose as we grow and experience Life in Time in this world of increasing speeds, addictions, and constant distractions. However, this is not to say that we could never regain this seemingly lost ability. In fact, we still have the ability to be Mindful. It's just that you have to "Be" in the moment, and too often we keep missing it.

Anyway, I believe that whatever it is, be it our own physical bodies or the things around us, they have very little to do with our thoughts. As I've said before, you can be physically here in the Present, while your thoughts may carry you as far back into your past as you can remember or as far into the future as you can imagine.

Thinking about our natural ability to shift our thoughts, I wondered if it is possible to be "Absent-Minded." Have you ever heard the phrase used before? It means to be habitually inattentive, preoccupied, or forgetful. All the same, the Mind is thinking about something even when it may need to pay attention to something else happening at the time. Are children Absent-Minded? I don't think so. In the phrase itself, though, there is the suggestion that there is an "absence of thought"—a state that I believe is virtually impossible. I know because I tried to clear my Mind of any thought through Zen meditation and did not succeed. I was preoccupied with the *thought* of clearing my mind.

I have heard of Monks and other Meditators who could clear their minds for moments at a time and it may simply be because they have spent years exacting their meditational prowess; they are the exception. The rest of us are always mindful of or distracted by something else. Otherwise, we may be fast asleep, in a coma, or dead.

It is when we are trying to get the attention of another, it seems they're in a trancelike state and unable to lend us the attention we want. Still, we should not jump to the conclusion that we are being ignored. It may be that they're presently "Being" mindful about something other than what you would like to have their attention for. It may simply be an "Earth to …" moment.

I'm almost sure you have experienced calling a child, maybe your own, while they were watching TV or doing something they're absorbed in. You could be right next to that child and they would not answer. Obviously, it is not that the child is deaf. But that did not stop you from asking them if they were.

What I believe happens is that you and your voice are outside their "Now," not their hearing. It is as if Time had an echo of its own and there is a delayed reaction from the Time your voice sounded to the Time the child heard you and responded and that's if they heard you at all. You see, the child is "Being" mindful as *they stay a moment or two longer in their Now, in their Bubble of Time.*

I don't know if it has always been this way with people paying or not paying attention. What I do know though, is that, more than ever before, we live in Times of increasing speeds and constant distractions. It is easy to see why it could be difficult to be "Present-minded" long enough to appreciate, even our own presence in this Living moment.

Fortunately, we now have available to us, the knowledge and the practice of Mindfulness Meditation. We can now make a conscious and intentional effort to be mindful and able to actually experience our own "Being" in the Present, in the Now, as we journey through Life.

With children, this apparent lack of attention is not limited to sound; it also involves sight. How often do we see children run into things when they're playing? I've seen it happen to my own children and I can remember it happening to me when I was a child. I believe this happens simply because children are naturally

Mindful (Present-Minded). I imagine this is why, as a child, I had the same experience. I would bump into things and it had nothing to do with being blind. It had everything to do with being in the Moment about what I was doing. *It's like being two steps behind the "Present," at least mindfully, or splitting an Instant in two. It's was like the "Thing" bumped into me a half of an instant before I realized it.*

Anyway, it may all simply be dismissed as kids being kids, and it's partly true.

Moreover, as children grow in Time and learn about numbers, their reference accumulates with the increase in knowledge and experience. They interact more with more people, places, and things and their horizons expand. There is talk about the past as they remember. There are plans for a future as they envision. Their minds do more and more thinking and these thoughts shift them in and out of the "Now." Of course, this is all perfectly normal for us as Human beings, Thinking beings. After all, we are intelligent.

Perhaps there is still something to being a kid at heart. It's true, we, as adults, or as God's children nonetheless, should not lose touch with the child in us, and I say this because we do. However, let us agree that this is attributable to adults having the knowledge, experience, and responsibilities a child does not have. To complicate matters, there is the constant assault of distractions, addictions, and the ever-increasing shuffle of speed and choice in a Modern era.

Meanwhile, we must be mindful that, just as our children are ours to raise, so are we, as "adults," children of God, who must continue to grow, learn, appreciate, and search for meaning in our own lives. We must always acknowledge the child within us and we should take him or her out to play more often and with more people. However, when we do, we should be mindful of our childhood way of staying in the *present moment for as long as we can, while doing whatever it is we're doing.*

Remember, there was a time when staying in the "Now" came naturally to us. However, now staying in the present moment is not enough. We should also be mindful of our "Being" in the "Present Positive Tense," for it is only "Now" that we can do something about almost anything, and what better state of Mind is there? Try, as often as you can remember, to "Be" mindful and aware of the seemingly obvious—that Life exists only in the Present, only "Now," and just "Being" alive is absolutely positive, but living with purpose and passion is positivity in motion. Otherwise, Life in the past or in a future only exists in our thoughts and as far as the past is concerned, it is obvious there is nothing we can do to effect change. However, we can think about a future "Now" with hope and positive expectations, and live and plan accordingly. We can be "Adult Children" who have the ability to intentionally slow down mindfully and physically for a couple of seconds at a time from Time to Time. We just have to choose to "Be" that way.

Before I close this chapter, I want to tell you a quick story about the "Cameraman" and the enigma that is Time. I've heard testimonials from people who have had near-death experiences. Perhaps you may have heard some yourself. They spoke of actually seeing their entire lives flash before them even though the experience lasted only moments, only instances. An example would be a traumatic event like being in a car crash.

I have been in one and the whole thing seemed to have happened in slow motion. Has this ever happened to you? Have you ever heard someone else say the same thing?

I remember one day, driving away from a Laundromat with my girlfriend and her daughter. As we approached a curb, I glanced at my girlfriend and noticed she looked tired. I leaned over to kiss her and right then she screamed, "Look out!"

I turned around and shouted "*Oh shite*!" but it was too late. We were already airborne and over a 50-foot cliff. The car rolled over repeatedly until it stopped right-side-up at the bottom. As the car rolled over, everything seemed to be happening in slow motion.

Of course at the time, it did not occur to me that my whole life was not flashing in front of me and perhaps it did not because I was totally focused on my girlfriend and her daughter. Maybe if I had been alone in the car it might have happened. Otherwise, the explanation may be that this phenomenon has something to do with our instinct of self-preservation, I don't know.

Anyway, while the car rolled over and over, I was able to brace my girlfriend's daughter from being ejected as she was propelled from the back seat toward the front, while at the same time holding back my girlfriend from being slammed into the windshield. It seemed as though I had all the time needed to do these things even though it all lasted only a few instances. It was as though the cameraman (God) was filming it all in slow motion for me to see. Now, why is that? I wish I knew, but I don't. It's not that the speed of Time had decelerated; that's not possible. Well then, Time being the constant that it is, could it be what I believe is a psychological defense mechanism we all have that gives our reflexes time to react in crisis? At the least, it seemed that way to me. But now that I am thinking about it, it is no more complicated than what I've been talking about all along, staying in the moment a second or two longer. The difference here is that in a car crash or other sudden and traumatic event, we go into autopilot mode. There is only time to react or, realistically speaking, there is only reaction in Time. Reacting in Time was the only thing in my entire life upon which I was focused. There were two choices available to me, do "Now" or think about a Time outside Now. Fortunately, the experience forced me into autopilot and I stayed in the "Now" for the one or two seconds I needed to protect my girlfriend and her daughter. I believe it is the enigma of Time, and it is as simple as that.

Now, staying in the moment for a couple of seconds longer in non-crisis situations is the challenge I propose to you. It is an ever-present challenge even though most of the time we are OK and unaware that the challenge at all times exist. It is a simple challenge, but not an easy one—yet, it can be done.

I have found that the best approach to handling such events, traumatic or not, is through the practice of Mindfulness Meditation. It is the best way to experience a fresh awareness of our "Being" mindful as we are and as everything is. With regular practice, you may experience a new appreciation and understanding of "Being" alive in the Present. I live this experience every "Now" that I am being Mindful.

By the way, we were not wearing seatbelts—big mistake. Instead, I had to play the role of the belt, and with a helping hand from the cameraman, we escaped with just a few scratches and bruises. On the other hand, perhaps we were just lucky.

INSTINCT AND ANXIETY

I believe animals have more of an instinct for Life than a concern for Time. I do not know if it makes a difference to them whether there is a Past, a Future, or a Present. Is a concept of the past and the future necessary for their survival? I don't know. However, I believe that natural instincts coupled with memory and experience is. Otherwise, they go about their lives simply surviving in Time. We do the same; however, for us as intelligent thinking beings, we do have a concept of Time, a past, a present, a future, and yet knowing there is only one Time, Now.

How about a baby? Yes, a human child. I suppose the same is true for the animal and the child in its infancy, when it comes to Time. An infant has no concept of Time. It simply exists as a living creature needing to be cared for, otherwise it will die. A child has instincts of its own. It knows how to suckle on a breast, whether it is their mother's or that of another lactating woman. But it is not enough for survival. All its instincts let it know that it is being cared for as its needs are satisfied. When it is hungry, it is fed. When it is cold, it is warmed. When it needs to eliminate, it does.

The infant has no concept of the past or the future. It does not even have a concept of Now. This it will learn in Time. Yet, as with us all, the infant's entire life is being lived in this Present, in this Now. It learns about Time as it grows, and soon enough, the child learns words like "when," "now," "yesterday," and "tomorrow," words that connote tenses. Still, learning these words and understanding the duration of Time relative to the Present are two different experiences. For the growing child, Time seems to drag along at a snail's pace. Meanwhile, for the rest of us, Time seems to fly.

Take a familiar example: I remember when I was still a child, even on Christmas Eve, Christmas still seemed so far away and couldn't come fast enough. Perhaps it was my lack of understanding and appreciation that caused me to perceive that Time had overslept.

Now, as an adult, Time seems to fly by, especially during the good times and to slog along during the bad times. Experiences like pain and suffering get our undivided and immediate attention. We're forced by those circumstances to become extremely sensitive and mindful of our "Being" in the moment as we are so affected. This is when it seems as though Time has slowed, keeping us in the Present for however long the experience lasts. However, the reality is that Time is a constant whether we are having fun or suffering. It is just that pain and suffering is not desirable and all our energy and thoughts are geared toward eliminating, or at least alleviating the condition "Now." There is no "Thought Surfing" when we are in the heat of the moment.

On the other hand, when we are having fun or just feeling good, our minds are free to enjoy, wander, and imagine all that is good about life "Now."

However, at some point, it dawns on us that the fun and the good feelings will not go on forever. It is a matter of Time now and these thoughts pull us into the future by the anxiety they incite, and so Time seems to fly by.

Why is it that when I am not in a hurry, it seems that everybody is speeding, and when I am, it seems like everybody is driving slowly? Why is it that when we want Time to speed up that it seems to slow down, and when we want Time to slow down, it seems to fly by? Of course, it is all about our perception of the fluidity of Time. For the child I mentioned, Christmas morning could not come fast enough, while for many of us, the weekend flies by too fast.

Not to worry, the true test of life is one we can pass if we learn about and practice "Being" Mindful. It may determine the difference between how well you enjoy the good times and how well you endure and survive the bad times.

Life is good most of the time, but Time is not mostly on our side. *Time is an equal opportunity spender, and at a time unbeknown to us, we're spent into "Nothingness" or into "Something" we know nothing about.*

Meanwhile, our thoughts and perception of the passage of Time do not alter its duration or speed. Still, who wants the fun to end? Not me. Who wants the pain and suffering to end? We all do; "Now."

When it seems we spend more time in the Present, I believe it is because adverse circumstances force us to pay full attention to "Being" in the moment. On the other hand, when it seems we spend less Time in the present, it may very well be because our thoughts too often shift to the future even before the fun ends. Perhaps we can blame our subconscious clock for that. It could be closing Time at the club or the party coming to an end, the final scene of a movie, the last song of the night, the ride home, or the last instant of a goodnight kiss.

As I said before, Time itself is not the issue. *It is our thoughts, understanding, anxieties, and acceptance of Time as being a constant in our lives and of Life as being a finite experience lasting but an Instant.*

WORDS MATTER

Do you believe words matter? Of course they do, whether they are spoken, written, or in Thought? The question has been repeatedly asked in conversations all over the country recently. However, why the question? Is it to draw attention to the prevailing national discourse?

Unfortunately, too many people hear but do not listen and it may because it is easier to hear (it is involuntary) than it is to listen (voluntary). Listening requires Thought and Thought requires the use of energy, and too many people are just lazy or too distracted to think about what they hear or read. On the other hand, some people are just mindlessly or outright biased. It is easier to rely on opinions and conclusions arrived at by "Talking heads" whose aim is to persuade their listeners to adapt their point of view. Furthermore, just as many speak simply because they have the ability to talk and not because they think about what they say before they open their mouths. Then, there are those who intentionally incite negative emotions with carefully crafted words that are wicked and intended to move others to act insolently and even violently. The saving grace here is that most of us choose to use words that engender Human kindness.

Suffice it to say the obvious: We use words to communicate with ourselves and with each other. We use them to describe the world we live in and the life we live. I also believe that most of the words we use are in our thoughts. Yes, we think with words and we are always thinking about something or the other, about the future, the past, and not often enough, being Mindful in the Present. We think more often than we speak. With me, it was the words, "*Life lasts but an instant,*" that dwelled in my mind for months.

Words can be used as tools, keys, or weapons. We use them in combination and sequence to open minds and to capture the imaginations of those we try to persuade. Words not only matter, they are powerful and can be used to move others to do "good," "evil," or "nothing." We also use words to heal or to hurt. Words like "I love you" and "I'm sorry" comfort and bring people together. Other words, perhaps not fit for print, can start a fight between two people or a war between two nations. Some of the words used in our culture are so negatively powerful that they are repudiated when used in full text, like the "N" word, for example. Its use is so egregious that it can get you fired from your job. Other words used in full text, like "Fire" and "Bomb," can cause fear and panic in certain situations. In fact, you could end up in jail for using these words.

Yes, the Fifth Amendment has its limits. However, I'm glad to say that most of the words we hear and use in everyday discourse are, for the most part, decent, caring, and loving. On the other hand, out of consideration for others, we keep many words to ourselves. As you know, *some things are better left unsaid.*

By the way, there is a word I became aware of only after having written it hundreds of times in this book. It is a word that encompasses all that matters and one we say almost automatically and on a regular basis. Actually, I previously mentioned two others, and as with the one I'm to write about, these words are usually used in greetings and in partings. The first is "Safe" and which I have substituted for the word "Alert" (a mindful cue) and the second is the word "Fine" used in greetings as an abbreviated response to how we are actually doing. The word I first referenced at the beginning of this paragraph, is the word "day." When someone said, "Have a great day" or "Have a good day", I would respond in kind. But then I gave this some thought and it occurred to me that these parting words referenced Time; a good or great "day". Of course, these parting words are good to exchange with each other and I encourage it. However, in keeping with the spirit of my thoughts about Time, I have substituted the word "day" with the word "Life". Now, I say or respond, "Have a great "Life" and when I do, people pause as if to do a double take. Try it next time and you will see what I mean. It is not what they are "accustomed" to hear and that's Ok.

Here are a couple other parting words I hear too often and makes me wonder: "God bless". Is this a fill-in-the-blank moment? Should I infer that the person asks God to bless "Me"? Why not use the next instant and say "You"; "God bless you?" All it takes is one more word, one more syllable to say what you mean. Just say it! God bless you.

Now that I got that off my chest, I digress. So far, I have yet to be told "Have a great Life" and when I am, it would be very much appreciated.

Think about it. Telling someone to have a great "Life", while living in the instance of their entire lives, is to speak to the truth of their present and continuing reality; not just this day. Remember, we are *ALWAYS* living our entire lives in the present; in the Now. So, the next time you share parting words, say "Have a great Life", for "Life" is indeed a great word. It describes all that matters and sharing it in parting words, I believe, is another idea worth spreading, don't you? Have a great Life.

The insatiable beast I spoke about is a formidable wordsmith. Like us, it has the liberty to be as deceptive, divisive, and destructive as it wants to be. *Caveat emptor,* this is Latin for "buyers beware." In this context, however, be mindful what ideas you buy into, *what words you let capture your imagination.* Keep an open ear, open eyes, and an open mind to the powerful suggestions that permeate our society. Question the "Talking heads" and don't be lazy. Think! Think now! *Think for yourself!*

Presently, is it as obvious to you as it is to me that tomorrow and yesterday do not exist? By now, you should know the answer. I've said it a thousand times already. Life does not exist in the future or in the past, and as far as the past is concerned, there are only memories of you, other people, places, things, and life lived.

We create an imaginary future with our thoughts based on hope, belief, and expectation. The past is the past—period. However, when we talk of the future or the past, the word "is" is often mistakenly used. Besides being bad English, it goes against my thoughts about the Now, about Presence.

Anyway, there is something here to think about. For example, it is common speech to say, "Tomorrow *is*...." next week Thursday *is* my birthday, etc. In fact, the word "is" cannot express ideas or imaginations of a Future even if it is a moment from now or of a Past, even if it was a moment ago. The word "is" must only be used to express Presence in the Now because there is "Nothing" outside the Now. All Time, all things, and all of us can "Be" no other Place or in no other Time but right here, right now. Only as time elapses does destiny become the reality of the life we "are" living "Now." *Only now can the word "is" express presence. Only now does the word "is" express the Present Living Moment.*

This brings me full circle to my understanding of Mindfulness as I described it in the beginning of the book, as living in Ism. *Ism is living in harmony with what it "is" and not what I wish it to "be." In other words, think of Ism as Perception looking into a mirror and seeing Reality for what it "is."* So it is with "Being" as I am and as everything is without judgment. I see the world for what it **is** and the world sees me for who I **am**.

Again I digress. As you know, words have been abbreviated for a long time now and their use is a matter of convenience. Acronyms are another short form and they too have been used for a long time. However, I find that the use of acronyms, often enough, is more for speed than for convenience. Besides the media employed by the insatiable Beast I talk about, it also has its own dialect. I call this dialect *Acronymese*. *FYI*, many of us speak this dialect on a daily basis. It is just that up until now you may not have known that it was a dialect and that it had a name. *OMG*, do not tell me you still don't know what I am talking about?

Anyway, I am somewhat alarmed about it all. Because it appears that the Beast will continue to rule the day and continue to tighten its grip on us. Fortunately, for those of us who choose to slow down, "Be" mindful and in control, we can continue to speak *long sleeve* English, *LOL*. For now, though, I would rather move on to the main topic of the day (Life in Time) than to discuss the intricacies and pros and cons of Acronymese. It would require *TMI* since it is not only comprised of combinations of letters but also of numbers, symbols, and Emoji.

Still talking about Acronymese and words, what do you think of this one: =qual (equal).

Anyway, here is a favorite acronym. What crosses your mind when you hear someone say, "Thank God it's Friday" *(TGIF)*? First, the odds are six to one that today is not Friday. If it is, did you thank God? If it is not, will you be giving thanks when Friday comes around?

To those who subscribe to TGIF as I once did, I especially want to talk to you. I pause when I hear people say, "Thank God it's Friday." It makes me wonder if those who TGIF also thank God for any other day of the week. If you don't thank God for any other day, ask yourself why not. I asked a friend this same question and he accused me of being too literal. "It's just something I say when Friday comes around. It is a way of expressing a sigh of relief that the workweek is almost over and that the weekend is here. It is about Happy Hour! It is Time to party!"

"That's all well and good," I replied. "But is it just something you say that has no meaning, or do you mean what you say"?

In other words, are the thanks you give God a sincere expression of gratitude or just something to say? I believe that words matter. When you say "Thank God it's Friday," are you giving thanks that it's Friday, or are you giving thanks that you are alive on Friday? "Both," you say?

OK, that makes sense because Friday would have no meaning if you were not alive to experience "Being." Then, let me ask you: What about Mondays? How do you feel "Being" alive on Mondays? "I hate Mondays." "Oh God, not another Monday!" Do these laments sound familiar to you? You may have uttered them yourself. I have. Other laments are censurable, outright indecent, and not suitable for print. You too probably know what they are.

Think about it for a moment. Just two days prior, you may have given thanks to God that it was Friday. So what is wrong with this picture? TGIF has become a national chant, just as "I hate Mondays" has become a national lament.

Sadly, I run into people who actually have bad Mondays for no reason other than it is Monday. I am reasonably sure that these same people have had bad Fridays too. The truth is, just as bad things happen to good people, so do bad things happen on days we celebrate, like birthdays, holidays, Christmas, Valentine's Day, anniversaries, and yes, on Fridays.

In other words, any Time is the perfect time for good things or bad things to happen. It is just Life and it happens all the time any Time.

Fortunately, the so-called Ordinary days vastly outnumber the days we celebrate, and so more times than not, good things and bad things will happen on ordinary days. I say "so-called" Ordinary days because I do not believe there is actually such a thing. A day is a reference to a period of time, and Time just *is*. Time is attributable to nothing.

So, don't just wait around for a particular day or numerical Time to celebrate Life. Celebrate life as you live it—right here, right now. "Be" mindful that if something good has happened or is going on in your life right now, let that be the icing on your cake.

What about Tuesday? Well, Tuesday for many is just one of those ordinary days. Its dawning does not incite emotions one way or the other. Tuesday is typically silent and almost anonymous. It tiptoes quietly by as it sneaks up on Wednesday. So, what is it with Wednesday? For most of us, it is the middle of the workweek. We like Wednesday so much we have given it a nickname: "Hump Day." It signals you have reached the summit of the workweek and that you're on the descent to Friday. For me, I can only imagine sitting atop a Camel's back and looking out into the horizon and hoping that what I am seeing is not a mirage but, in reality, Friday. Think about it: Wednesday is the only day of the week with a nickname. Perhaps it is fitting that we also thank God it is Wednesday (TGIW), what do you think? By the way, Latinos like Wednesdays too and have their own nickname. It's called "El Ombligo de la semana": The Navel or "Bellybutton" of the week.

Then, over the Hump and upon our descent, we step into Thursday. Thursday is like Tuesday except it is a day of anticipation and we like it more. So much more that I think Thursday should get a nickname too. What do you think about this one: "One more day"? I hear it almost every Thursday in the office. Yes, Thursday is the "One more day" day. Do you like this nickname? It is what you hear on Thursday mornings at the work place or at the office. "One more day. I can't wait." It is the fourth day into the Camel ride toward Friday. It is the "mental rubbernecking" of people trying to get a glimpse of Friday. Thursday is the eve of the "working holiday" that is Friday. Then at first light, the nation chants, "Thank God it's Friday!" Most of us show up at the office in a relatively good mood, especially if it's payday, and saying what else? TGIF.

I have never heard anyone complain about having to work on Fridays. Perhaps it is because most of us take it easy while our Minds shift gears and as Time elapses toward five o'clock.

I do not know if there are statistics about productivity levels at the workplace on Fridays, but I would not be surprised to find out they are relatively lower than Mondays. At least it seems that way at my office. Anyway, most of us cruise through Fridays. Then it is off to "Happy hour" or home for two days of rest and relaxation; at least that is usually the plan.

In Puerto Rico, celebrating Fridays is a cultural event. It is called "*Viernes social*" (Social Fridays), a time so many look forward to. People meet at their favorite "watering hole" (bar or lounge) for a drink or two. Happy hour on Fridays in Puerto Rico is not just a couple of hours hanging out with co-workers and/or friends and sipping on a favorite beverage. It is a cultural affair.

Most of you know about the famous TGI Fridays restaurants; it was one of our favorites. My daughters and I used to like to go there for the fun and food. By the way, now that I think about it, I do not recall ever going there on a Friday.

All in all, I think it is a good thing to get together to share in the good Times. Most importantly, though, I believe that we should use the Life we have, whether it is on Friday or any other day of the week, to celebrate Life as we have it and as we are. Otherwise, I think it is sad to focus on the days of the week ahead of us or even the past, whether positively or negatively, because when we do, we miss the Present Living Moment and all that *is* going on. It is so easy to miss this Moment, this Now. *It goes by instantaneously.*

As a side note, here is a little history about how five days of the week were named. It was the Ancient Greeks who named the days of the week after the sun, the moon, and the five known planets, which were, in turn, named after the names of the gods Ares, Hermes, Zeus, Aphrodite, and Cronus. They called the days of the week, the *Theon hemerai*, "days of the Gods."

Monday was named after the ancient Greek God hemeras Selenes: "day of the moon." Tuesday: hemera Areos, "day of Ares." Wednesday: hemera Hermu, "day of Hermes." Thursday: hemera Dios "day of Zeus." Friday: hemera Aphrodites, "day of Aphrodite." Before Now, I did not know this. Now we know.

Here is a fair-minded question: "What if I hate my job?" Before you answer, let me ask you this, "Do you hate your Life?" I bet you don't. If you did, any day of the week, whether you hate your job or not, would be a perfect day to feel miserable, right? Fortunately, most of us do not hate our lives, at least not every facet of our entire lives. As you know, there will always be Times we dread. Just the same, there will always be good times, Times we live for. Then, of course, there are the Times we celebrate. However, good Times or bad, *living through them is more about the attitude you have about your present existence and the realization that Life is merely a temporary state of "Being."*

We should always try to be mindful that since Life itself is a temporary experience, so are the good Times and the bad. Fortunately for most of us, most of our lives are good or, at worst, simply uneventful and routine. As a matter of virtue, we should all thank God for the bad Times and not just for Fridays, but also for all the good Times. The bad Times in life, and how we survive them, are what gives flavor to the good Times. They deepen our appreciation for Life, and the pursuit of happiness becomes a worthy and exciting Journey.

Here are some old childhood sayings I remember, maybe you know them: "You can't know what's sweet if you don't know what is sour. You can't know what is hot if you don't know what is cold." You get the point.

BEING, THEN DOING

Living is all about *"Being"* then *"Doing,"* and as simple an idea as this may sound, it can be complicated. What can, and usually does make it complex is our ability to *travel* mentally, and when we do, *much "Doing" goes undone.* Our thoughts shift back and forth from the past to the future and back to the present. I call this "Thought-Surfing." In fact, we spend most of our time thinking outside the Moment, outside the "Now." We're usually thinking about what we have to do next. Right now, I'm thinking about what it is I want to write. In between moments, I'm thinking about how long I will continue to write before I go to bed. As you can imagine, I am sitting here writing, but my thoughts are about the future, about what's next. I'm here physically in the Now, but my mind wanders and it's OK; it is what the Mind does. I need only to gently rein back my thoughts to the Present, to what I am doing as I continue to write.

So, what about "Now"? Nothing, except to be mindful and aware that it is the only Time I "Am," the only Time I can "Be," and the only Time I can "Do." In terms of attending to the meaningful things and persons in my life, I must "Be" mindful of my own presence if I am going to be able to appreciate all that is happening as I am and as everything "Is" without judgment.

Now, I realize that I cannot devote all my energy and thoughts trying to stay in the Now. Actually, it is impossible. *"Time" is a nonstop train we board as we are born and we ride until we run out of Life. This is when we disembark into the other side of Time and literally disappear into the Past.*

During the ride, we have our entire lives to live and that means we have to continue to think about and plan for a future. I've heard people say, "Don't dwell in the past." I've uttered those same words myself. However, when we say them, we are suggesting a shift to thoughts about the future. But isn't the future Now when we talk about past? The answer is yes, but only in thought. Otherwise, all Time is "Now" and for that, I thank God. TGIN.

All thoughts about the Past or the Future can only occur in the Present, in the Now, and I realize you know this. Moreover, we have to wait for Time to elapse as the Future becomes "Now," again and again until we run out of Life.

So then, because all Time is "Now," what do we do? This is a great question and the answer is that we should 'be doing' what is most important or necessary at this Time while "Being" aware and mindfully present as we *are* and as everything *is*.

If you are at work, you should be working, so put away the book for now. If you are in a class, then you should be listening to the lecture, not reading. Make it your intention to set aside your own Time to read. It could be "Now" O'clock at night before you go to sleep or Now O'clock in the morning. Just to keep things simple. Whatever important thing you should be doing, do it now. This is not to say that doing "unimportant" things is necessarily a bad thing, no. We need to escape from reality from Time to Time. Some fantasizing, daydreaming, and even doing "nothing" is good. The reality is that we live during very high-stress inducing Times and we can all use a break, a Mindful respite.

Still, when I am working, studying, or doing something important, I can't say that I spend every instant being mindful about the task at hand. *I travel in and out of the Now with my thoughts*, and as I said before, it is what the Mind does and it's OK. Still, I have to get things done, and so I gently draw my attention back to the task I should be mindful about and continue.

Moreover, because we cannot escape the Present, we may at least be positive in the moment. We should always strive to stay in the *"Present Positive Tense," at least a moment longer, and while we are, we should be thinking positively.* Now, here is something to think about. *"Positive thinking is a Mind Style that can lead to a great Life Style. Meanwhile, embrace the Present with the hope of a great Future. File the Past."*

A DEFINITION OF SUCCESS, GOOD FORTUNE, AND GOALS ACHIEVED THAT NEVER ARRIVED TOO LATE

I really do believe that the achievement of our goals, or good fortune for that matter, never arrive too late. If, at the time, you have life and the mental capacity to know and appreciate what it means, it arrived just in Time.

To begin with, success means different things to different people and most define it as, "the achievement of a goal." I have a different view. The way I see it, I could not have achieved my goals without experiencing Success. On the other hand, I could experience Success without having achieved my goal. Of course, I would prefer to achieve my goal. Who wouldn't? If I didn't, surely I would feel disappointed, yet not defeated. To feel defeated or that I had failed, I would have to disregard the "Journey," which was necessary to achieve my goal in the first place.

"It's about Results," they say, the embodiment of things tangible like a new car, house, a trophy, or maybe even a yacht. Then, there is the new job, technique, becoming a published author, earning an advanced degree, or peak awareness through Mindfulness.

Tangible or not, the world identifies us as being successful because of these embodiments or statuses. However, rare is the recognition of what was involved in the commitment to endure the Journey, a journey paved with hard work, sweat, tears, sacrifice, intermittent wins and temporary setbacks, stress, frustration, anxieties and disappointments; A journey traveled with positive expectations of a goal to be achieved. Fortunately, this recognition is our own, our own Success, our own Living experience. This book is an example of an embodiment.

One thing all successes have in common is that they all began with a single thought, an Idea, and with this idea in mind, a commitment to pursue followed. It is with a commitment, forged with passion, purpose, confidence, sacrifice, and a specific intent to do those things we believe would make the idea a present reality some "Now" into the future. This is Success, and it makes the achievement of a goal probable.

When it comes to ideas, I have a curious Mind and if an idea crosses it, I try to find out why it did and what meaning it may hold. As you know, some thoughts just simply occur to us. They seem to come out of thin air ... or do they? Sometimes I try to make sense of an idea, but soon enough I forget about it. It doesn't interest me, I get lazy or it just slips my mind, and who knows what becomes of it. It may be absorbed back into the ethos or it may enter the mind of someone else as a "Thought" occurrence.

So, what happens to that idea? Am I the only one who knew of this idea or is the idea like a seed that drifts in the stream of our collective consciousness and in Time seeps into the mind of someone else who makes sense of it? You see, an idea, original or not, can be like a rough diamond. If you came across one, you may pick it up, look at it, and then throw it away. It looks nothing like the *faceted* gem (diamond ring) offered upon bent knees in the proposition to marry. Rough diamonds are carefully cut and polished by people specialized in doing that kind of work. The same is true with ideas/thoughts. When an idea occurs to you and you don't ponder its meaning, you may, one day, find yourself on bent knees crying, "Why didn't I think it through?" Perhaps you or someone you know may have had this unfortunate, yet learning experience.

In writing this book, my hope is that one or more of my Thoughts may be a rough diamond you can cut and polish for use in your own life. Whether the thought is an idea to start a business, write a book, invent a new product or start living your life in search for new meaning or a fresh perspective, I strongly encourage you to go for it. Just keep in mind that it is all about the Journey, your own Journey, embarked upon and being mindful that *the meaning of any Thought/Idea is in the mind of the Thinker—so "Think."*

Before I continue, I would like to share my definition of Success as I "Feel" it. Success, to me, is a series of emotional experiences lived while in the pursuit of a worthy goal. It is living with intention, confidence, passion and purpose; this is what the "Journey" is all about. Paradoxically enough, the achievement of the goal does not matter as much as you may think. I'm talking about Life here, and as far as the Journey is concerned, what matters most is that the experience of Success is an indispensable and necessary precondition for acheivement.

For me, as I believe it is with you, Success is deeply personal and only I can feel it. No one can experience it for me. Just as well, the same is true about feelings of disappointment.

Here I am suggesting that, even if the goal is not achieved, one can be successful. Having said so, I am mindful that, for many, failure to achieve a goal means one is less than successful. I disagree. It doesn't change the reality, value, and importance of the life you've lived while in pursuit of your goal. With this in mind, my meaning of Success also suggests that one cannot fail in terms of life lived while in the pursuit of a worthy goal. This Life lived should never be thought of as a waste of Life, a waste of Time, a waste of Lifetime. It is to be mindful that it is all Life, Life best lived.

For those who believe not achieving a goal makes you less than successful, perhaps this quote may give cause to reflect: *"Think of Failure as nothing more than a temporary experience. It is not a permanent condition or a terminal disease. Experience it, and then let it go. Survive it and try again. Nothing scares away Failure more than another Try. Nothing is more attractive to Success than Courage, the courage to try again."*

When I set upon the achievement of a goal, it is with the belief that I can achieve it; otherwise, I would not act. I would not make the first step. Then, when I decide to act, I admit there often seems to be a lurking feeling of the fear of Failure. If I recall correctly, the late Zig Ziglar was the first to use the word "FEAR" as an acronym to inspire his readers and listeners when he talked about the pursuit of goals. He said that FEAR is simply ***False* *Education* *About* *Reality***. When it comes to reality, it is always Now O'clock and the fear of failure is a real and present emotion triggered by thoughts of an imaginary outcome of some event some Time in the future. The concern then becomes how to allay a present Fear that may very well stop you in your track. Well, a quote reads: "It's all in the Mind," and in many cases, I believe this is true, especially when considering the future or the inevitable.

So, how do I get rid of a present Fear of a future outcome? My answer is simple: recognize and treat the Fear for what it really is (a mind shadow) and accordingly "Be" open to new perspectives and move forward anyway.

Now, I don't want you to think this is easy for me to do. It is not. We're talking about emotions here and there is no on/off button that you can simply press. Nevertheless, for me, it was Zig Ziglar's acronym, FEAR, that inspired me to think of the feeling of "Fear" in a different way. Now, I am mindful of two things. The first is to accept that Fear is a real and present emotion, and second, that it is based on an imaginary outcome sometime into the future, which is not presently real. So, with a change of perspective, I began thinking about fear as a "pending" anxiety as a way to regulate my emotions, which in turn made it easier for me to think of positive outcomes moving forward.

As it is with many things in life, a change in perspective can make a difference; it has for me. Keep in mind that Perspective is in the mind of the Thinker.

Now, I pursue goals with what I recognize as an "anxious anticipation" about a future positive outcome. Anxious anticipation is my own perception, my own Mindfulness about outcomes, and this mindset seems less stressful to me.

Something else I seriously consider when I commit to the pursuit of a goal, and it may be more important than anything, is that I do not disregard all other facets of my Life. I still live my entire Life as I go on about pursuing my goals, and I do so mindful of "Being" in the present, when leaving anything out is impossible. The present reality of my life, and yours for that matter, is that it is always *whole* in the Now.

Furthermore, it is vital to me that the quality of life I live as I pursue my goal be nonetheless meaningful and satisfying; it may as well be. It is all part of my Journey, a Journey that begins as it ends until I run out of Life, my whole Life.

I believe Life is a Journey mostly fueled by emotional experiences that, as best I can, I try to regulate through thoughts and perceptions. I also believe that life's pursuits, however sophisticated or simple, are temporary episodes (mini-series) experienced during the Journey that is my *entire* Life.

Here is another quote to ponder: *"The Thrill lives in the Hunt, but dies with the Kill." The Thrill is about making the most of your life while in the Now; you may as well. We are all "Traveling Hostages" of the Present as we journey through Life in Time. Then there is the Hunt, the intentional pursuit of a worthy goal, an episode interwoven into our lives as a whole, and culminating with the Kill, the goal achieved and the reset of a new goal."*

S-U-C-C-E-S-S

S – <u>Serious</u>: The pursuit of a worthy goal should be treated as a serious endeavor.

U – <u>Unstoppable</u>: You should be passion-driven as you pursue your goal. Don't beat yourself up if you encounter setbacks. Press on with anxious anticipation.

C – <u>Committed</u>: A high degree of commitment is required if you are to achieve your goal. Realize that *"Attaining many things in life is much easier than making the commitment to actually attain them."* In the words of Zig Ziglar, you have to be the "Bacon," not the "Egg" in a "Bacon and Egg" breakfast. Here the chicken is merely involved but the pig is committed. You see, the chicken can always lay another egg. But, the pig gives his life so you may have bacon. Now, that's commitment.

C – <u>Confident</u>: Confidence and positive expectation is what keeps us moving toward our goal. It is what gets us out of bed in the morning. It is what pulls us into the future with anxious anticipation.

E – <u>Enthusiasm</u>: Of course, you will need to have the "get-up-and-go" to get to where you want to be. However, don't expect anyone to share a drink in your vision of a successful journey toward your goal if your pop has no fizz. Fizz is the enthusiasm gas that exudes from the passion you are driven by and it can be contagious. You will need that gas because you alone cannot achieve your goal, others will be involved. However, to get others involved, it will take enthusiasm to capture their imagination and get their trust to journey with you toward your goal, a goal only you can envision. Keep your Emotional tank filled with Enthusiasm gas.

S – <u>Smart</u>: Know what to do and what steps to take. Follow directions, figure things out, seek advice, research, etc.

S – <u>Satisfied</u>: You should be satisfied as you actually achieve your goal. You should also be satisfied if you have done all that was required and did not achieve your goal—it's Life. The Universe does not always conspire with us, and it may be why we don't always get what we want even having done all that was required or expected. Still, the time and the experiences lived will never be in vain. It is your Life lived. It is one of the many episodes of your life and being qualified to say, "I gave it my best," talks to the Journey, your Journey, and the series of emotional experiences lived. A worthwhile Time of Life lived.

Rest assured that you will always be older tomorrow than you are today and, hopefully, with age, experience, and wisdom comes a contemporaneous appreciation for future "Nows" and all that will be happening in your life at the time. Remember, to really appreciate any experience in the "Now," you will need to be fully aware and mindful that you are "Being" as you are and as everything is: *goal achieved or not.*

Here is a Success story. It was newsworthy to tell of a woman well into her 60s who had gone back to school to get a law degree, and yes, she achieved her goal. She spoke about how happy she felt and how the sense of accomplishment gave her a new outlook on life. Is she talking about her entire Life and the experiences lived during her pursuit of a Law degree? Of course she is. In her late-60s, it was not about starting a Law practice, though she would offer her service. For her, it was all about the Journey. It was about how she felt on the way and at her arrival at her Present Living Moment. It was about her awareness of "Being" in her own presence—then and there, goal achieved.

Like this fine Lady, we should all be mindful that it is about being aware we are always living our entire lives in the present and about how we feel about ourselves in the Now. Is it not what life is really all about, *a fresh sense of "Being" at your destination in the Present Living Moment, here and Now?*

In a similar vein, and as I mentioned before, being told by a Judge that if I had not made "it" by the age of 40 I would never make it; that it would be too late. We were talking about me going to Law school. He also said he didn't think I could be a good

Lawyer because I was the compassionate type and to be a good lawyer you had to be dispassionate. Well, I did not go to Law school and it had more to do with the present reality of my life and other interests I had on my mind than being dispassionate. I was already a Realist.

Regardless, whether your pursuits begin at 15, 30, 60, or 90, what will matter most is how you are feeling about yourself on the way and upon arrival at your Present Living Moment, and so long as you have life and the mental capacity to know, be aware of, and appreciate, you will have arrived just in Time—not a Moment too soon, not a Moment too late: arrival Time, Now O'clock.

Here is a story about good fortune. A 73-year-old woman had the good fortune to win a multimillion-dollar lottery. She was overjoyed knowing that she could now put her grandchildren through college, give to her favorite charities, and cover her last years of care so as not to burden her family. Just imagine what her last "Nows" were like. Her good fortune arrived when she still had the mental capacity to know, be aware of, administer, and appreciate her good fortune. I am sure you can think of a few other stories, yours probably being one.

The bottom line is that our entire life is a Journey. Everything we do, think about, every heartbeat and every breath we take is all part of the Journey and it is all contained in check-in luggage and carry-ons as we travel in Time and in pursuit of our goals. *Long-term goals are what I consider check-in luggage and they can seem monumental if we lose sight of the "Now." Carry-ons are things I need to do and can do now during my pursuit of long-term goals. Then it is only a matter of Time before I arrive at my destination and actually live my dream, as the Future becomes my Present Living Reality, as I continue to live my entire Life, "Now."*

However, before I begin to pursue a particular goal, I always have a plan. *A plan, like a map, is a written instrument used to get me from where I am now to where I would like to be some "Now" into the future. Without one, only God knows where I will end up.*

Furthermore, I believe that *all my plans must die if my dreams are to live. But, for plans to die, they must be executed.* Meanwhile, I must be persistent yet patient, for patience is what flavors the pursuit of goals.

If you do not have a specific goal in mind, consider the following: *To reason that each of us is unique, is to reason that each of us now possess at least one gift or talent. However, the discovery of that gift or talent is exclusively reserved for those who purposefully seek it out; some find Success this way. Still, not everyone believes they possess a gift or talent and so do not have reason search. Regardless, always try to be mindful that there is not, there never was, and there never will be anyone better than you, at being "You"; you're already the best. Of course, we should always continue to strive to be better.*

Then there are times when having done everything we set out to do to achieve our goal, we still encounter "Failure" and there could be a number of reasons why. For starters, there are those things or events we have no control over. Perhaps, it could be because, as I mentioned before, attaining *many things in Life is much easier than actually making the commitment to attain them.*

I've heard it said that the achievement of a goal usually involves at least two people and this has been true for me. The following quote is a good reminder. *"When two people come together to work on an idea, three minds are present: yours, mine, and the fusion of ours."* This is to say that things get done simply because someone believed in the *"self"* and in someone else and when both believe, creative ideas and solutions are born. These ideas and solutions are not orphans but fruits of the minds of those who come together to Think. This kind of belief inspired by leaders can capture the imaginations of the minds of those they lead and thereby harness their cooperation for a specific purpose. Imagine three minds. Imagine the exponent of the minds of an army of 300.

Still, on the subject of Goals, obviously it is impossible to know how a future "Present" will be like. We can only hope it will be as we imagined or according to plans we had made. Either way, it remains impossible to know. However, it is certain that we will be older, likely wiser, and that's about it. Will we be healthy enough to enjoy the fruits of our labor and live an active Life, a quality Life, a fun Life? We just can't know. Will your husband, wife, children, or friends and family be around when you achieve your goal? Will nature, as we know it today, be the same? Will wars and climate conditions worsen? Will the cure for Cancer be made available to those who can least afford it?

These questions are impossible to answer today, to answer now. So, exactly what are we working toward and planning for 10, 20, 30 years into the future?

Only Time can reveal the answers to some of these questions. In the meantime, however, try to be mindful that *as you walk through Life and toward your goal, keep your eyes on the next step you make. You do not want to step into something unpleasant.* In other words, focus on your Journey now, not your goal. Be mindful and aware that your entire life happens in the Present, in the Now, and that barring the unforeseen or the unexpected, you will get to your goal or destination as Time elapses. *It is more likely that, once you have made the first step into the Mile toward your goal, you will always have less than a mile to go. So, do not stop now.*

I am reminded of the following motivational quote—whose author is unknown to me—that drives home the same basic point: *"The difference between a Big Shot and a Little Shot is that the Big Shot was once a Little Shot who just kept on firing."*

Still, it is so important to make the most of the Journey in the *Here* and *Now, even while pursuing your goal.*

Also, be aware that the person you are now, as you set your goal, may not be the same person some five, 10, 20 years down the road. Life experiences may actually change your perspective on

Life itself and even the goal you had set out to achieve. I certainly am not the same person I was five, 10, 20 years ago. My Lady Friend and Juan Massa had lamented to me that they now believe they would have been happier, healthier, and more fulfilled with less work, less money, and more Time actually living Life *Now* ago.

However, I still believe it is not necessarily a matter of less work or money. The lesson here, I believe, is a matter of living a consistently balanced Life as you pursue goals. Remember that life is all about "Being" as you are and as everything "Is," preferably in the Present Positive Tense.

In life, you may not always get what you want, no matter how hard you have worked or how well you have followed your plan, and it may simply be because, at any given moment, there are so many variables we have little or no control over. This is why it is so important to remain mindful of our "Being" in the "Now" while appreciating those with whom we share our lives. It is to make the most of Life now until you get what you want, and if you do not get what you want when you want it, you will still be in a good place in Time. I do not think I could emphasize it enough when I say, *"Being" in the Now just a little longer is so important. It is all the Time you would need to slow down and breathe a little more Life into your Now.* It is a moment to be mindful that a goal is just that, a goal. It is a vision that exists only in your mind even as you live your entire life in this *"Now."* As they say, "Savor the moment," it may be your last drink of Life.

After all is said and done, here is something else to keep in mind: there are at least five billion people in the world who would trade their lives for yours without caring to know what your life is about.

WE CAN'T KNOW, WE MUST NOT KNOW, AND THANK GOD IT IS SO

I expect to live for some Time to come, and so the future is usually on my mind. However, I do not use a lot of energy thinking about it. Instead, as I journey, and from Time to Time, what I do is take a mental peek out into my horizon to make sure I'm on the path toward my goal. It's sort of like taking a quick mindful glance at a check list and immediately crossing out tasks already accomplished. Meanwhile, I'm here and now with thoughts on my mind and hope in my heart that I will actually be living the Life I had planned for and imagined. Nevertheless, I am aware that the reality is that sometimes the life we imagine remain dreams that never come true. If this has happened, or if it ever happens to you, don't allow yourself to be discouraged. *Just be mindful that it will always be better to have dreams that don't come true than to not have any dreams at all.*

Like everything else in Life, we dream in the Present and our thoughts about our dreams are all part of the reality of our entire life and that is a good thing. Just thinking about them is positive, and thinking positive is "Being" positive in the Present Tense and in the instance of your entire life. Thoughts about my dreams and goals make me smile more, and I'm usually in a better mood as I anxiously anticipate achievement.

I'm like the child whose Mom (Destiny) told him that he would get a candy from the candy jar tomorrow(Future) if he continued to be a good boy, work hard, and be patient. Unbeknownst to Mom however, I'd hidden a piece of candy in my mouth and smiled to disguise what I'm up to.

We know that Life is about enjoying the moment, a small taste, a sip of the Life you dream to live tomorrow, today. Think of it as "Life-tasting" while on your journey toward the candy jar. Before you know it, you're at the end of the rainbow when the taste of the candy is sweetest, goal achieved and living the goodness of your new present reality.

Of course, during our journey through life and, as it is in any equation for Success, there will always be variables we have little or no control over. Some of those variables may be related to health, family, economics, and/or nature and even when we plan for the unexpected, the possibility of being blindsided is always there. Life happens and the Universe does not conspire with us; it's as simple as that. What then? You don't quit for sure is "what then." I instead, treat being blindsided as maybe a signal from the universe that I chart a new course, modify my plans, or simply lower my expectation just a little. Depending on my circumstance, these changes may be just what Dr. Destiny prescribed.

Nevertheless, I believe it is wise to be prepared, to be mentally nimble in any event because we can't know before "Now" which alternative will be available and best for our lives at the time. At all times, however, be mindful that Change is a chronic and inevitable side effect of the Constance of Time. With this in mind, it is important to consider that the further into the future your dreams live, the greater the likelihood the unforeseen or unexpected will pop up. This is true for the journey that is Life, a long road trip, a five-year goal, or a 50-year marriage. Murphy's Law has nothing but Time on its hands.

So we live as we do today with our beliefs, attitudes, hopes, principles, and values, characteristics that are part of our makeup and integral to any equation for Success. It is about who we are and are becoming, moving forward.

Now, depending on our age, circumstance, and our total reference at the time we make our plans, some or all of these characteristics may change altogether as Time elapses and Life happens. This, by the way, may not necessarily be a bad thing. Regardless, after having achieved our goals, we will not be the same person who had some years' prior, set out to attain them; *we will* **always never** *be the same twice*. I mean this literally.

Of course, we can imagine or even visualize ourselves in a future, and this is a good exercise for goal setting. Still, we can't know for sure if our goal will be met and our dreams realized. We just don't know. We can't know, and thank God, it is so. Not being able to know is why it is wise to always make the best of life "Being" in the Present Positive Tense while on your journey, whether you have a goal or not. Remember that Life is a "Present Tense" experience and that the future is a Thought experiment.

Still, remain mindful that realized dreams involve changes to our lifestyle; it comes with the objective. The achievement of your goal may afford you a fancy car, an expensive house in a nice neighborhood, private school for your children, and other "Embodiments." The question then becomes, "Did my beliefs, attitudes, principles, and values hold throughout?" Only you would know that. Yet, you're not alone. We all change in Time and with experience, whether we're goal oriented or not.

You may have heard it said about someone or perhaps yourself, "Since they became a doctor/lawyer or the boss, they are not the same person as before." But, of course not, that is what change is all about whether natural or volitional. Obviously, we can't avoid natural changes like aging, the unforeseen, or the unexpected. On the other hand, our pursuits, as difficult as they may have been, may not be more difficult than actually living with the benefits. Sometimes, it is easier to achieve a goal than it is to live with what the achievement affords you. Your achievement can have an effect on the people you associate with, positively or negatively, and sometimes these people are friends and family and it could be challenging. It's OK though; it is usually what change does. Just keep in mind that it is "your" Present experience, an experience you have made come true. Also, realize that at the same Time, associates, friends, and family are living "their" Present experience and that eventually everything else will fall into place. It's only a matter of Time.

As humans, we are designed with the ability to think as we are with the inability to know the future, and I believe this is for the good of Humanity. I certainly am thankful to God that I cannot know my future. I believe it would *devalue* the present Moment, the only moment there is, the moment in Time I live my entire Life. We already do a lot of "Thought Surfing," the kind of "Flash Thinking" that only results in many missed moments, moments when our ability to appreciate the Present is missed. But that's not all, because to miss the moment is to miss your entire Mindful Life for the duration of that moment. Think about it: We are moving so fast, constantly distracted and "Being" oblivious to the many and costly missed moments in any given day. Imagine how many Lifetimes that could amount to. Nevertheless, it's a *"loss of living"* expense we do not have to incur every time. Here again is where "Being" as you are and as everything is without judgment can minimize the losses. Slowing down and paying attention in the Here and Now will always be more valuable than knowing the future, regardless of what you imagine it to be. After all, it is only in the Present Living Moment that you can experience your own presence where and when you will always "Be" before you can even begin to dream, much less live that dream. This is why the Present is so precious. It is all the Time we have; it is all the Time there is. So, savor the moment more often than you do now. There is always Time for another sip: Cheers!!

Consider this Thought experiment: What if you knew of an imminent danger to yourself or a loved one and there was nothing you could do to stop it? What would you do? This kind of "knowing" could paralyze you mentally and/or kill you right then on the spot: time of death, Now O'clock!

Still, not knowing the future is simply being human. It is still OK to imagine what's around the corner, the boogieman under the bed, or to dream beautiful dreams even if they don't come true. *You will always have "Now" to "Be" as you are and to "Do" as you will.*

When you think about it, five, 10, 20 years ago, you could not know your life to be as it is now. Still, you're here and I bet you're OK. Now, keep in mind that I am talking about who we were and are becoming as humans and not about the Things we planned for and may have accumulated over the years. It is one thing to put a plan in motion in order to acquire a Thing sometime into the future. We could start saving dollars to make a down payment on a house or buy our dream car. It is quite another thing to set out to be true to who we are now and our thinking about who we will be at some point into the future. Still, we just can't know; we must not know, and thank God it is so.

To be sure, our total reference will continue to increase as we live in Time experiencing our "Being" in the Present Living Moment as we are and as everything *is*.

Mindful that *Life lasts but an instant*, I like to think of my Tomorrows as gifts, gifts I open every morning when I wake up; gifts that are always mirrors. When I look into my mirror, the reflection is always different throughout the day every day throughout my Lifetime, and I like that. Of course, I am talking about what's most important, the reflection of my Mindful "Being," not my physical image.

Meanwhile, we all have our daily routines, the many minor decisions we make subconsciously. Then there are major conscious decisions we make. We join a gym, buy a house, or get married, and after we're settled in, routine and all, the force of Life happens. There is a sudden tragedy, the diagnosis of a deadly disease, divorce or the loss of a loved one, and we're compelled to make difficult decisions. Life's happenstances such as these are what many of us have had to cope with and we are, or we did.

Ordinarily, when we take it upon ourselves to make Life-changing decisions, they usually involve variables we never contemplated and, perhaps, at the time, may not be able to manage. All of a sudden, routine goes out the window and something new and powerful is in your face. I have heard it put this way, *"It is one thing to know the devil is out there somewhere. It is quite another when he knocks on your door and ask for you by name."*

Fortunately, for most of us, we believe we can take on any challenge Life may visit upon us and it is good to think positively. However, remember, we are talking about the Future. We're talking about a Time that exists only in our thoughts as we are in the Now. We know who we were and, for the most part, who we are. But, we do not know who we will be tomorrow and whether we would, in reality, be able to cope with the cards Life deals us.

Thankfully, for most of us, Life has been and is mostly good and that tomorrow, again, will be a good day. Still, from Time to Time we should do a reality check by "Being" mindful that we will *always never* have lived in the Present moment before now; the reality is that we are always living on the edge of Time when, in this undiscovered frontier, what is next can't be known. We must not know and thank God it is so.

HER LAST BEST FRIEND AND THE LIVING MONUMENT WE CONTINUE TO BUILD FOR HER

Here are a few questions no one has ever asked me and how Life forced me to answer when I was least prepared. What would it be like to let pass an opportunity to do something special for, or say something kind to someone and it was your last chance to do so? What if it was for someone you truly love?

First, let's be honest and agree that opportunities abound and are freely available to us and that perhaps this is why we take them for granted. It's not that we don't care, at least not on our side of the equation. But, what about the other side, the one you love? Do missed opportunities go unnoticed; perhaps? It may depend on what side of the equation you're on at the moment. Regardless, we are all present in the abundance of opportunities to be Human kind. It's just that our pace of life and the constant distractions make it easy to miss the Moment. Consequently, too often we let opportunities go by without saying something nice or doing the right thing and then it's too late. This we should be mindful about because there may come a time when we let pass an opportunity we may live to regret, an opportunity that will have passed forever, yes *forever*....

Family members of wartime military people and law enforcement officers are particularly vulnerable to the loss of this opportunity. They face this reality every day as their loved ones go on about their lives doing what they do best. For family members, there is a palpable anxiety about their return home after they have worked their shift or served their tour of duty. In their case, the unexpected and unforeseen loss of a loved one is devastating, heartbreaking, and permanently life-changing. Of course, in the overall journey of life, anyone may suffer this experience.

Still, who is to say that the next moment will not be your last? Who is to say if the next moment will be the last for the one you love? Statistically, it is not likely that this moment may be your last, but it has to be someone's last moment. It is for many, and just like that, in an instant, it could be yours or mine.

Sometimes in Life, seizing the opportunity to say or do the right thing may be beyond our control. Then, there are times when we are in control and still let it pass. Listen, some small things in life make a big difference when we are "Being" mindful of those we love. To say, "I love you," "I'm sorry," "Thank you," or "Goodbye," to visit or to help or simply be there, are opportunities we could lose forever and that loss could be regretfully overwhelming. In such cases, there is no makeup test, part two sequel, or second chances. There is only regret and I'm here to tell you, regret is one thing you do not want to live with, losing a loved one is sad and hurtful enough.

I lost my beloved wife, Marilyn, and my children lost their loving mother. For a year and a half, she fought a courageous fight but succumbed to lung cancer. Her looming death was relentlessly painful, dreadfully slow, and tearfully sad. We were all heartbroken. Nevertheless, we got the chance to *"Do" for her, to "Love" her.* We loved her very much, very often, and in all the ways she needed and wanted to be loved until she ran out of Life. Loving her had nothing to do with us being in a good mood, rested, tired, sad, or even sick, and we were all that throughout the ordeal. Every day, we wore the sadness and the stress like heavy lead jackets. But it was all about loving her in spite of the emotional roller coaster we were always on.

Tried as I did, it was difficult to stay in the Now because thoughts of test results, doctor visits, emergency room visits, Chemotherapy treatments, medication schedules, and the undying hope that Mom would get better soon were all thoughts about the future. These thoughts were always present and we could only escape them for moments at a time. Nevertheless, the Loving was always *on and in the Present Positive Tense.*

It was about 5:30 in the morning when the hospice nurse woke us up to let us know that my greatest love, my daughters' Mom, was about to run out of Life. As we stood over her, we could see that she was not physically responsive. However, during her last few labored breaths, we believed she could hear us; she was still "here." My daughters and I, with eyes full of Cry and hearts heavy with sadness, got one last chance to tell her that we love her and that we would miss her very much. We told her that we knew she loved us and that we understood that she was (dying) running out of Life. We each kissed her and said our last goodbye just as she had taken her last life-giving breath.

The night before, I had whispered in her ear that I had spoken to Amada and Bianca and explained that Mom was going to die. I told her that she could go and that the girls would be OK, that we would be OK.

I got the sense that Mom held on as long as she did in the end days because she wanted to know, to be told by me, that the girls knew what was about to happen and that they would be OK.

Like you perhaps, and many others in similar situations, we were conflicted with feeling very sad that Mom had run out of Life and that we had lost her forever, while at the same time feeling "glad," she suffered no more. For my beloved wife and the mother of our beautiful daughters, *Death was her last best friend.*

She was finally free from her broken body as she slipped into the *Eternal awakening on the other side of Time, in heaven.*

I remember the day before, a man visited us. To this day, I do not know who he really was. I think he was from Hospice and may have been a doctor, but he talked like a pastor. That afternoon, we were in the dining room and I was sitting on the table, while he sat on a chair. I remember that he spoke softly and with sincere concern about what we were going through and what was to come. He seemed to be counseling me. From where we were, we could see the most beautiful human being I had ever known as she laid on the hospital bed that Hospice had provided. The man said, "You see your wife there, right now she is seeing the face of God and heaven. She is seeing children at play, beautiful flower gardens, and angels." He said that she was 25% "here" and 75% "there," already in heaven. I just listened. However, I got the sense that he wanted me to believe what he told me about my wife. Instead, what I came to believe is that in times of grief, those kinds of words comfort and console, and that's a good thing. We are human, after all, and the right words or just good words at the right time can rouse the kind of emotions that help us cope with sickness and accept the loss of a loved one. At least for a few moments I felt a sense of peace.

After the man left, I got my girls and hugged them closely and tightly. I wanted them to feel the peace I was feeling. Still, we were not OK—not for a long time.

A few days before Mom ran out of Life, I became concerned that her last Moment would be on a holiday like Thanksgiving or Christmas. I did not want that to happen. I did not want her memorial to fall on a holiday. I also did not want her to run out of Life at home, even though it was what she would have wanted.

Looking back, I see that my thoughts were scattered and my emotions fractured. I was drunk with fear, anger, anxiety, and sadness. However, somehow I was able to sober up and realize that home is where she belonged and where she deserved to be until her last "Now." It also occurred to me that it should not matter what day she ran out of Life and that instead I should be mindful that she would always live in our hearts and minds every day, ordinary or holiday.

It was Tuesday, November 2, 2005, the day of Mom's last "Now"; it was one of those *ordinary days* I talked about. I later learned that in Mexico, November 2 is when they celebrate the "Day of the Dead." *What a twist of fate*, I thought.

My beloved wife Marilyn ran out of Life with grace, beauty, and dignity. During the time I cared for her, I made some of the right decisions and it had to have been God who made the others for me because, a lot of the time, I was emotionally inebriated. I have been at peace with Mom's absence ever since, and so have our daughters.

Today, I reflect and I don't know which is worse, losing someone to a long drawn-out ordeal with cancer or in some unforeseen and unexpected way. I realize that a loss is a loss. But, for me, there is at least one special difference and it is having the chance to say the things you would most like to say or do the things you would most like to do before you or your loved one runs out of Life.

This is why I can't emphasize enough that "Now" is the only time you have to do or say anything.

Still, I'm not suggesting that you Love someone every moment of the day. Sometimes we're not able to seize the opportunity even when it's available. What I am suggesting though, is that you love more often because we never know "when" ...

For those who find it difficult to move beyond grieving, always be mindful that *"Time" still "is"* and that *"You" still "are"* on this side of Time.

I understand and appreciate that we grieve and it is a normal and healthy characteristic we have as human beings and some grieve longer than others will. However, as best you can, try to always be fully aware that *you are in the Now; a Time beyond the Life of your late loved one.*

Fortunately, for most of us, there are others in our life we can love and be loved by, as there is Life to do so now. I implore you, *"Don't get used to grieving." I say this because you can, and because this to may be regrettable. It could cause those who love you and have moved beyond grieving the same loss, to now suffer that you haven't.* Stop for a moment and really think about what you just read.

We should all try to make a conscious effort, after a Time of mourning and as soon as we can, to begin to focus on how best to honor a loved one who Time has left behind. Start by moving on as you know they would want you to. *Make the story of your Life moving forward, a Monument to the memory of your late Love.*

In our case, we know that Mom would want me to get back on the golf course and that Amada and Bianca would continue doing very well in school and have fun and healthy lives. In memorial, this is our way of continuing the Love we shared as a family. Our monument to Mom is a Living Monument. We're constantly evolving as better human beings, and even as Time spends us, we are well on our way.

You know, I never got back on the golf course because I soon realized just how much of my life I now had to dedicate to our daughters. They had just turned 11, five days before Mom slipped out of her broken body and into the other side of Time. My life was different now and I had to adapt new perspectives and shift priorities.

I did what needed to be done and to the best of my ability and with all my love. Our daughters continued to do well in school, graduated Summa Cum Laude from the International Baccalaureate Academy at their high school, awarded full scholarships and are healthy and very busy being college students and having lots of fun.

You know, it is only because of the love, care, and teachings Mom gave the girls while they were the "Three musketeers" that my part going forward was made easier. Mine is an undying gratitude to my wife, my Marilyn, my Love: "Thank you honey." Now, we believe that Mom is pleased and smiling with us all the time.

We should always try to be mindful that we cannot "Do" anything else or anything more for those we loved who have run out of Life. If we are to love, and we should continue to do so, we should love those who are still among us, here and now. For my daughters and me, our loss was great, painful, and sad. I lost the best thing that had ever happened to me. I lost a loving wife and a beautiful human being. Amada and Bianca lost the most loving and caring mother any child could ever wish to have. I love my daughters, not just with all my heart, I love them with all my Being and I will always love them *"Now."*

For us, the idea of spending "Quality" Time with each other is about the sharing of our thoughts, conversations and the affection we have for each other, lots of kisses, hugs, and "I love you."

Here, two elements are in play and being mindful of them makes living a whole lot better for me. The first is Time; the *highest quality element* there is and second is Life, the *highest state of being. As one simultaneous experience, I am "Being" fully aware, and mindful as I am and as everything is without judgment.* It helps me evolve into "Being" a better human as I continue to Love now and Love much.

I've said before; it is impossible to spend Time. Instead, Time spends us. For us, all Time, every Instant, every Now, being the only Time we live, is "Quality Life in Time."

As Time passed, it was revealed to me that *as much as we had lost, we were still left with so much; our glass was still full.* We have each other; we have Angel Luis, my beloved son, their beloved brother who was with us and by our side throughout and beyond Mom's ordeal. His love was an extra special sanctuary wherein his sisters found shelter from the rain of sadness and ease from the uncertainty they were feeling.

We also have Titi (aunt) Dahlia and Uncle Pete, grandma, Malulu, Herman, Tete, Patricia and Frankie. They were the only ones who were there for the girls, and it is why I think of them as Pillars of the living Monument we continue to build for Mom.

Still, there is so much loving to do, and even if we lived a thousand years, we could not love them as often and in all the ways they deserve to be loved. Lucky for us, at home, we have each other to love and we do love each other every "Now." *We now know it is true. Time is not just a great Healer, but also a Truth Revealer.*

HOW I TRUST GOD, THE MIRACLE OF LUNA, AND THE BLESSING OF MIRACLE

We can't deny the reality that everything is ever-changing as we continue to evolve as "Thinking Beings" during the unending passage of Time. Moreover, as thinking Beings we should be fully aware and mindful that because of this reality, it is inevitable that we are always becoming more of our "Self" in terms of our mental and spiritual growth while simultaneously becoming less of our physical self. It's just what Time does.

Therefore, as far as the effects of the passage of Time are concerned, it seems to me that the evolution of our collective Mind, our thinking, continues to outpace the deterioration of Matter, which of course, is the makeup of our bodies. On the other hand, this phenomenon does not apply to you or me as single individuals, unless of course we left the world a markedly better place. Otherwise, when we run out of Life, our thinking ceases and our bodies literally disappear.

However, the Human race continues to persists and thrive because of the Collective Mind, the Thinking Mind, through thoughts that perpetuate our continuing existence.

Starting from the beginning of Life, the body of knowledge we now possess was once unthinkable, and it is from this body of knowledge that it is conceivable that it will continue to increase with new knowledge and new thinking about old knowledge; this, Time will allow.

Personally, it is easy to understand if you think back to when you or your children were born. We knew nothing; we had no knowledge about anything. Then, as Time elapsed and as we grew, we learned to say a word (Mommy) or two. Then we began to small talk, learn the 123s and ABCs and our empty minds quickly filled with new knowledge and corresponding reference. The rate of learning is so fast that some scientists believe we learned even when we are fast asleep.

From the beginning of our race, from our own individual beginning, we embarked on a journey of learning and using knowledge to understand our lives as Thinking Beings. Today, there is no evidence that the Human journey will end anytime soon and if it did, it may very well be because as a species, we became extinct and for no other reason.

Meanwhile, with knowledge comes perspectives and perspectives continue to shift and change with the evolution of our thinking about new knowledge as well with old knowledge and experience. For example, over Time, when talking about "Being" and living and Life, some things, though unknowable, determine how we live a faith-based life.

Generally, for older folks, Life takes on a different meaning. Naturally, spirituality and mortality become ongoing concerns. Thoughts of Redemption, Reconciliation, Death, God, Heaven, and Hell are on their minds. Seasoned citizens are aware that Time continues to spend what's left of their lives.

I digress here to remind you that we do not run out of "Time," we simply run out of Life. Furthermore, I dare say it is Time that makes us mortal, and being mortal makes Death inevitable. The natural equation (TNE) remains in effect. It proves that Life itself is a *subtraction* proposition. We do not get more of it. As Time elapses and Life is spent, there is no replenishment.

When I think about it, I thank God that I will run out of Life in a final Instant, some Now into the future. No, I don't have a Death wish. I have a greater wish and it is *some form of "Being" on the other side of Time in a place I now imagine Heaven to be.*

Because I am merely human and because I believe, I try to live my life by the "Ten commandments," or at least some version of it. As a guide, I believe it is a good way to choose to live. I call it "Heaven insurance," a way of living that serves as an insurance policy in order that I may benefit if, in fact, there is a God and a Heaven.

Come on, most of us are required to buy auto, medical, and homeowners insurance so that we may be covered in the event something bad happens. Still, don't get me wrong here. I am not suggesting that running out of Life is a bad thing. There is no way of knowing if the inevitable end of Life as we know it is a bad thing. What I do believe, however, is that the end of Life may lead to an extra-dimensional gate that opens into *the other side of Time*. It may be the gate through which we have to pass if we are to ascend or cross over into Heaven. Fortunately, for those who believe, God has allowed for a 98% discount of the price of admission. Death is the ticket that gains you access had you chosen to live a life "Being" a good Human. On the other hand, our investment in the covenant is only 2% in the currency of Faith in God, a mustard seed's worth. I don't know of a better deal, do you?

As I was saying, we buy insurance at great financial costs, behavioral modification, and knowing that the benefits are insignificant when compared to the promise of eternal residency in Heaven. While we're here though, we try to drive carefully, and we take good care of our health and property. Of course, there is much virtue in these behaviors and most of us derive some benefit at some level. On the other hand, we are not compelled to live by certain morals, principles, and values, and there may not be a direct or immediate financial cost to suffer. Still, we are free to be as nice, as considerate, as fair, as respectful, as loving, and as charitable as we choose to be; as well, we are free to be as bad-minded, inconsiderate, awful, and evil. However, because most of us believe in a God, we try to be as our God has asked us to be, or perhaps as we imagine God would want us to be like, on this side of Time.

It is not up to God whether we follow his commandments or whether we are good or bad. God designed us as intelligent beings with the free will to choose good over evil and right versus wrong. God has offered us all an open invitation into heaven and we gain entrance when we run out of Life having made "good" choices and lived faithful to Him.

For the next few moments, loosen your mental safety belt, open your mind, and take this detour with me. Even being faithful, I have the Human curiosity about what it all means and how it happens. Perhaps, you're just as curious. Anyway, I can't help but wonder if we all come into Life from some level in heaven. Is this thought so far-fetched? Think about it. We don't know where we come from or where we go when we run out of Life. Of course, for the faithful, God in heaven is what awaits them 180 degrees later. At least, that is what we hope and pray for.

So, let's go back to when it all began for each of us; when we were conceived. It is the first Instant of our lives, the miracle of conception, believed to be an act of God, God who resides in a kingdom called Heaven. It may be the beginning of our first journey through Life. Perhaps it is our second, third, or fourth journey through Life here on Earth. I imagine that, for some, the first journey would be the only one they have to take. This may be especially true for infants and for very, very good and faithful humans. For the rest of us, a second journey would be the first Trial during which Time we subconsciously redeem ourselves with the hope of rising to a higher level when we return to heaven as we run out of Life over and over again. Obviously, I have no way of knowing which journey I'm on. I should only hope that I'm on my second and last—who knows? Perhaps I've been here more than twice and now find myself on my last journey after which I will make it to the highest level in Heaven and won't have to come back here. Nevertheless, for those of us who have, and for those who will come back, it may be that we reincarnate repeatedly until we reach the highest level in the kingdom of Heaven—I don't know. Maybe I am just chasing thoughts as they cross my mind and trying to make sense out of the whole idea, but this we can't know; only God does.

In this stream of consciousness, it occurred to me to ask, does Déjà vu have anything to do with reincarnation? Could Déjà vu be what our soul's eye see as an instant transcendent glimpse through a hole in the gate of Time that God allows us, sort of a hint that we really reincarnate? Again, I don't know, but I remain curious. How about you?

Still, we are born, and then we live the way we choose to live until we run out of Life, and who knows what then. *I hope Heaven, in all its glory, is next for you and for me.*

I have to wonder if there is a universal Truth, and there may be, as evidenced by the common knowledge that most people in the world, past and present, believe in a God and in a Heaven. I also understand that most people believe that if they are to meet God in heaven, they must first die. In other words, *we must first run out of Life if we are to run into God*. Still, many resist even the thought of running out of Life and perhaps it is simply the fear of the unknown. But wait a minute, if you do believe in God and in heaven, aren't these also unknowns? I don't know God or anything about Heaven. However, like many of you, I just trust in God and that when I run out of Life, and having lived faithful to God, that I will be in heaven.

So how do we reconcile Fear with Trust? Those of us who say that we believe in God and hope to go to heaven may need to come to terms with our mixed feelings about first having to run out of Life. Fear of the unknown is one thing; fear of the inevitable is irrational, don't you think? So, how does one overcome such a fear? It is simple and it starts with being sincere about what we really do believe. To say that you believe in God and in a Heaven while at the same time having a fear of running out of Life reveals either that you really do not believe or that your trust in God may not be as strong as it could be, which is it? What is there to fear of eternal Love and Happiness in heaven with God? Either way, the reality of Life is that whether we believe or not, whether we trust or not, some "Now" into the future, we are all going to run out of Life, then what.

Two questions you may want to think about and answer are: What do I really believe, and, am I ready?

This story may inspire you to think about answers. At a business meeting, a longtime associate of mine told me that a close friend had died and that he spent the last night crying almost uncontrollably. It occurred to me to ask him if his friend believed in God and in Heaven.

"My friend had a strong faith in God" he answered.

"So why do you cry?" I asked.

"What do you mean?" he replied.

I said that I believed that when someone runs out of Life (dies) having a True faith in God, they go straight to heaven.

"My friend believes in God as much as I do and his faith is just as strong," he said.

"Well, knowing that your friend is with God in heaven is good reason to celebrate the life he lived and your own aspiration of joining him there later. Now, if your friend had died not believing in God, perhaps that would be reason enough to cry because he would be denied entrance into the Kingdom. He would be denied being there with you."

My friend replied, "I never thought of it that way. It makes all the sense in the world."

Still, life remains mostly an emotional experience, not an intellectual one, and so we will continue to cry.

Nevertheless, let's be real for a second. When we lose someone and we weep and mourn, is it because the person died, or that we no longer have that person in our lives? Could it be pure selfishness on our part? Either way, perhaps it is simply our Human nature.

In the meantime, live Now, be a good human, and do what you enjoy most doing. Love now, love much, love often, and let yourself be loved and your life will be a happier one. In such a life, there is little time for fear of anything, especially the inevitable; invest in Heaven Insurance. Don't be the one who drives through life with one foot on the gas and the other on the brake at the same time. Time will pass you by and you will run out of Life anyway.

As I said before, *Life is a perfect positive state of "Being" and it is something as opposed to Nothing.* Death may be perfect as well. But it is not known if it is positive, negative, or really "Nothing." We only know that it lies in wait as we run out of Life. But what is "Nothing"? My own definition is that *"Nothing" is the unthinkable and to think of "Nothing" is impossible. The fact is, to contemplate "Nothing" is in fact "Something." Perhaps the closest thing to "Nothing" is Death, something we know nothing about.*

To some, God is "She," and to others, God is "He," and for others, God is "Nature." Different religions have different names for God and different notions of what they imagine heaven to be like. Who knows what is true? I don't believe anyone does.

I speak for myself, as I say that I believe in God and in Heaven. For me, living a Life believing in God and in Heaven is a matter of Faith, of Trust. *I may die and find "Nothingness" or, hopefully, God in Heaven.* If there is Nothingness, at least I lived a Life of faith, service, consideration, love, and respect for my fellow man and that would be a good Life to have lived.

Still, for me, as my life is spent, *"Time" may have well been my Master, but God may yet be my King.*

Here I want to make an admission about my Trust in God. I have a real fear or anxiety. I am not sure which it is when it comes to having faith in God. It may be both. I have mixed feelings, but I trust anyway. It is the most difficult challenge I face all day, every day. When I pray about something, I know that I have to trust that my prayer will be received and answered; otherwise, why pray? Still, the fear and anxiety never goes away and there appears to be no way to reconcile the two emotions. For me, it is a constant balancing act, and trying to make sense of it is indeed challenging.

Now that I am writing about balance, it occurs to me that maybe the fear is that my prayers may not be answered at all, and the anxiety is being able to recognize and appreciate the form the answer may take. I say this because we don't always get exactly what we want, how we want, or when. I'm left to imagine that some of the answers may come in the form of a sequence of events over Time that would require patience and continued faith in order that my soul may see, as the answers *manifest* in my life. In the meantime, I continue *to trust God, do my best, be patient, and trust my destiny.*

As they say, "God works in mysterious ways," and as usual, for me at least, it is the battle between the head and the heart where Trust is the mediator. It is why I believe that I trust, because I realize and appreciate that most of the times throughout my life, whether I'd prayed or not, I've been and continue to be, truly blessed. I bet you feel the same way too.

Here is a story about something very special that happened to my family and me. It happened in a way I described earlier as an answer to a prayer that may have come through a sequence of events over Time and in a form different from what I may have prayed for. On the other hand, it may have been just another blessing bestowed upon us; I'm still, to this day, not quite sure.

At the Time, it was something I had in mind. However, I do not recall praying about it. Yet, it served the needed purpose as it manifested in our lives. This is the story of a blessing and a miracle bestowed upon us by God.

One August afternoon I had taken my daughters to JC Penney to buy school uniforms, and entering one of the dressing rooms was a woman with the cutest little puppy in her purse. I asked what kind of puppy it was and she said it was a Chihuahua. My daughters saw the puppy and were so excited and happy that right there and then it occurred to me to get them a pet. I asked the woman about getting a puppy and she said they had a female that was pregnant and would be having pups in a few weeks. She gave me her number so that I could call to arrange to get one. We finished shopping, and on our way home, the girls would not stop talking about the puppy. They were happier than they had been in a while. However, their feelings of happiness only lasted until we got home. That's where and when it turned to the daily concern and sadness we felt about Mom.

You see, Mom lived with feelings of despair and suffering every day all day. The pains were excruciating, and so much so, that the strongest painkillers like OxyContin only reduced the pain a degree or two and only for a short while.

As you already know, Mom was battling lung cancer and life had taken on a reality of pain, fear, sadness, and frustration. She was especially frustrated with the efficacy of the pain medication as it did not bring her the relief she wanted. The relief Mom wanted was for her to be able to continue to be Mom. She wanted so much to do the Mommy things she usually did for our beautiful 10-year-old daughters. But every day that passed she could only do less. She was also bothered that she could not be the wife she had always been to me, especially in terms of intimacy. It did not matter to her that I would say she should not worry about such things and that I was OK, that I understood. She wanted to be the mother and wife she had always been: a good wife, a loving mother. She wanted to go back to working as the great hair designer she was in spite of her modesty. Marilyn was the best thing that ever happened to me and she was the best Mom any child could ever wish for.

When Mom was well, she would take the girls everywhere with her. They hung out a lot and referred to themselves as the Three Musketeers. I loved it. I loved just knowing that my daughters were able to enjoy their Mom as much as Mom enjoyed them. We were a beautiful family in a home where when you walked in, you could tell that Love lived there.

Mom was the girl's own personal professional hair designer and Mom liked nothing more than making them look prettier. She also enjoyed walking them to school because it was only 10 minutes from home.

Then, there came a Time when Mom struggled to make the walk to and from school. By the time she got home, she was almost breathless and very exhausted. Lung cancer does that. However, Mom still had the energy to make the girls pretty. It was something she loved to do.

Eventually, that ability also faded with the spread of the cancer to other areas of her body. Most everything Mom enjoyed doing became more and more of a task until the only thing she could do was allow herself to be cared for. She had lost her roles as Mommy and wife. She was now the main object of our care and concern. This was to be the most stressful and heartbreaking stage in our battle against a deadly foe.

In the meantime, I had been calling the number the woman at JC Penney gave me. I wanted to know about the puppy, but got no answer. I called several times after and at different times of the day and no answer. I wanted so bad to get a puppy for the girls, but I had to abandon the idea.

Mom's condition was worsening and I had to be there by her side every free moment I had. I also became increasingly worried for the girls. They could see that Mom was not getting better and that she could not do Mommy things anymore. When the girls would come home from school, they would greet Mom with a kiss, ask her how she was feeling, and she would always say, "OK." Then they would get a snack, go to their rooms to settle in, chill for a little while, and do their homework until it was time for dinner.

I knew it was Mom's selflessness talking when she would say that she was OK. She did not want to worry the girls. By this Time, the mood in our home had become as sick as Mom was, and it didn't help that we too had become sick with concern for her. Home was no longer a lively place. It became mostly a quiet place where Love prayed.

Our lives were all about doing everything we could to care for and comfort Mom. It was the usual doctors' visits, Chemotherapy sessions, waiting for test results, prescription fillings, emergency room visits at all hours of the day and night, and frequent hospital stays.

One day in October 2005, the doctor told me that my greatest love and the mother of my daughters was now in her End days. At first, I did not understand what that meant. I was so tired, sad, afraid, and confused. But, my undying hope made me think the doctor meant that the cancer was in its end days, that we were winning the battle. At the same time, those words did not match how I felt in that moment. I had a sinking "gut feeling." It was like feeling three emotions at the same time, the numb feeling of a broken heart, a broken heart for whom Hope had chosen the "happy envelope" stuffed with sadness and sealed with fear. In that moment, I felt that my wife and I were dying together, but I had to be strong. I had to "Be" there for the girls. It was like being shot in the heart but still able to stand and walk only because something greater than my own life was more important: The Life of my wife and the wellbeing of our daughters. I believe the phrase I am looking for is "utter shock," a shock that never really subsided, not for a long time. My focus was on caring for Mom until it occurred to me that the girls also needed me more and more, especially seeing how Mom was rapidly weakening, mentally tired, and deteriorating emotionally and physically.

By this time, I had completely forgotten about the puppy, but my concern for the girls reminded me just how important it was to get them a pet. It would be a good distraction from all the sadness and stress. It would give them something to care for and something to play with. A pet would bring a little happiness into their lives. Home would at least be a little louder and livelier. But where would I start looking for a pet, and what kind? I got really frustrated because, more important, was the present and pressing reality of Mom's declining condition and the love and care she wanted and needed, now more than ever.

I believe in prayer and I prayed all day every day for Mom to get better. Like most people in similar situations, I prayed for a miracle. I also prayed for the strength to keep the girls as calm and assured as I could. I prayed for the strength to be able to endure and survive what was to come. What did not occur to me at the time was that, as selfless as she was, Mom also prayed for us.

With all that was going on, we were now faced with the imminent landfall of hurricane Wilma, a category II hurricane. On October 23, and during one of her hospital stays, it was "Discharge" day, but her doctor told us that she could stay until the storm passed. But Mom wanted to come home and so we brought her there. The following night, October 24, 2005, Wilma landed stronger than the experts had forecasted. It was one of the most stressful nights of my entire life. I was up all night making sure that everything was secured, Mom was attended to, and that the girls were calm. At some point, water from the force of the winds was coming through the bottom of the front door. I placed some towels but they quickly became saturated. Then, Amada came up with the idea to use Play-Doh. She gave me the Play-Doh, and together we applied it. I told her she was my assistant engineer and she liked that; we had a little fun together. The idea worked to save the night and bring down my stress level a notch. Now I could totally focus on caring and comforting my wife as Wilma blew through.

The following morning, I woke up, greeted my wife with the usual kiss and "I love you," made her some tea, and gave her medication. Sadly, this was the routine. By the way, so that she could sleep better, Mom had to be reclined so that she could breathe easier and the Lazy Boy in the family room gave her that ease.

Anyway, I went to check on the girls and they were still fast asleep. I quietly closed the door and headed outside to see what damage Wilma had left in her wake. As I stepped outside, the sky was still crying, but getting wet was the least of my concerns. A few steps outside, there were broken palm branches everywhere and debris and patio furniture in the pool. I did not know where to start the clearing and cleanup. At that moment, I felt overwhelmed by the whole mess outside and the sadness I was feeling inside.

I looked around and, in my despair, I asked God for strength. Just then, I could hear what sounded like kittens. I looked around but could not see where they were. I walked toward the sound and under some broken palm branches and at the base of two palm trees were three black kittens: triplets for our twin daughters. They appeared to have been born during the storm, and looking at them, I could not believe they survived the storm as well as they did. They were in very good condition. They were in what was like a pocket or cubbyhole at the base of the trees. There they had the protection they needed to survive the storm.

Before the storm, I had never seen a cat in our backyard. I was so surprised and excited to tell and show the girls. For the moment, I felt some happiness inside I had not felt in some time and it was because I knew the girls would be so happy to see the kittens.

I went inside and told my wife about the kittens and she smiled. It was all she was able to do with the constant pain she felt. Still, it seemed the pain she felt had subsided for the moment knowing the girls would be happy. Moreover, thoughts about how preoccupied they would be made her feel less sad going forward. It was all about being in the moment as she was and feeling that all was well in her world in the instance of her life, in her present living moment. Only God's medicine can do that.

I went into the bedroom, woke up the girls, and told them I wanted them to see something out back. On the way out, they greeted Mom, gave her a hug and a kiss, and asked her how she was feeling, and as usual, Mom said "OK"; this time she really was, but just for that moment.

By now, the sky had stopped crying as we stepped outside. The girls could not believe the big mess hurricane Wilma had made and for a moment they thought it was what I wanted them to see. When we got to the palm trees where the kittens were, I said, "Look babies!" They were now fully awake and very happy to see the kittens. Their faces lit up with "WOW!" I could see the happiness in their eyes as they asked if they could keep them. Of course, I said yes.

How could I say No to what I believed was a Miracle and an answer to a prayer I had not made, at least not consciously? That day in JC Penney, the idea of getting the girls "a" pet was born. Now, it had to have been God that gave them three.

That night, I had to take Mom back to the hospital because she was feeling as one in her condition would feel during the last of her End days: sick, afraid, and tired of being sick and afraid. When we got there, the doctor came to the room after Mom had settled in, stabilized her, and she fell asleep. Three days later, on October 28, 2005, it was the girls 11th birthday and we had a little celebration in the room with Mom. We were all as happy as we could be under the circumstances at the time, and then again, maybe we weren't. Five days later, on November 2, 2005, and in her own home, Mom slipped out of her broken body and into the eternal awakening on the other side of Time, in Heaven.

You know, God is great, merciful, and so loving that he will even answer prayers made or not. I believe it is God's way of blessing us simply for having faith in him. In other words, you do not always have to ask in order to receive; you need only trust and believe and God will provide when in need.

We were all in need of something that would lighten the mood in our home and so it was. God had lifted some of the weight I was carrying on my shoulders and he had eased some of the suffering my wife was feeling, at least for a few miraculous moments. It was God's way of showing mercy by bestowing upon us a means to cope with what was to come. At the time, I could not see the irony in this gift, but soon after, I did.

The three kittens had come when we most needed them and they had survived the destruction of hurricane Wilma so that we could have new life to care for, lives that came with a real promise and a new beginning.

Now the girls had something after school to come home to. They would rush out back to see the kittens and play with them. Soon enough they met Mommy cat and were even free to play with the kittens when she was there. This became a daily event for the girls and it served as the perfect distraction they needed to transition in terms of their emotional Being. It was the start of a life in Mom's recent and permanent absence.

Soon enough, they decided to name the kittens. Amada named one Jonathan, Bianca named the other Luna, and they both agreed to name third one Scrabbly.

By the way, there was one condition about keeping the kittens; they could not feed them. That way, when they grew up, they would leave, and so it was.

Sometime in April 2006, the kittens were all grown up and left as I expected. However, now I had a new problem. The girls started to miss the cats and I had to do something about it. I thought about the woman and the Chihuahua puppy, but I remembered throwing away the phone number she gave me. So, I started a Chihuahua "puppy search" and it quickly became frustrating. It seemed they had become extinct.

My son Angel Luis was also in the search party and early one evening he called me to say he was at the grocery store and outside was a man selling Chihuahua puppies. I told him to get me the man's name and number. Listen to this, the man's name was William. That same night I called William, went to his house, gave him $200 and came home with the cutest brown and black 10-week-old Chihuahua puppy. I felt blessed and was so excited for the girls because it would be a loving surprise. Fortunately, it so happened they were at Grandma's for the night. I could bathe the puppy and it could begin to get used to me and to our home. Then it occurred to me that it was the night before the first Mother's Day without Mom and a bittersweet feeling came over me. Just then, Puppy jumped off the sofa and appeared to have hurt her leg, but I did not give it much thought.

Now, it was Mother's Day morning and I had more of a sweet thought in my mind than a bitter feeling in my heart. On my way to Grandma's, the thought of my darling little girls being so happy to meet their new pet was greater than any bitterness I might have felt in my heart. When they saw Puppy, they were so happy they could hardly contain themselves as they fussed over who would hold it first.

When they finally put Puppy down, they noticed it limped when she walked. I told them what had happened and it was then it appeared the injury was worse than I thought and so we took her to the Animal ER. An X-ray revealed that Puppy had fractured her little leg, and of course, I gave the doctor the OK to treat Puppy. Then it was an all-day wait for the doctor to fix Puppy's leg, cast and all. It will be a Mother's Day we will always remember, a day that was mostly about Puppy, not Mom, a day that was mostly sweet, a good day. We thanked the doctor and his staff, stopped by Grandma's for a little while and went home. That night the girls agreed to name Puppy "Miracle." Perhaps, they should have named her "Miracles."

By the way, one day all three cats showed up and the girls were so surprised and happy to see them and play with them. However, it appeared they had not come back to stay. Maybe they sensed the girls had a new pet and wanted to see for themselves, who knows? After a few days, only two would stop by and then there was one, Luna. How the girls knew it was Luna might have been a Twin-Triplet telepathy thing, what do I know? Anyway, eventually Miracle and Luna became friends until she too left only to stop by once in a Blue moon and, perhaps, just to say hello.

So you know, I had hoped that Miracle would be a Teacup. Fortunately, she grew no bigger than what I call a "Coffee cup" Chihuahua. Still, she was smaller than Luna.

And so it was, and as I believe it is with God's blessings upon us on this side of Time, blessings that are answers to prayers made or not made and whose purpose is more important than form. I wanted a puppy for the girls and God, perhaps testing my patience, gave them three kittens first. However, at the Time, I was not aware of any sequence of events, nor that I was being patient. I was simply "Being" and "Doing" what I needed to do to keep our family whole. Meanwhile, I was mindful of the trust I had, a trust I wavered on at times but never lost. It was trust that allowed my soul to see as the answer *manifested* in our lives in the form of a miracle that came in the dark of night and in the wake of a natural act of destruction, named hurricane Wilma and later followed by a blessing named Miracle.

We continue to have a strong faith and trust in God's will as we are lifted, carried, and moved until we, too, run out of Life and slip into the *eternal awakening* on the other side of time, in heaven, and for us, hopefully with Mom. In the meantime, I continue *to trust God, do my best, be patient, and trust my destiny.*

TRAINING WHEELS AND A LESSON ON RESPECT

For the second Time in my life, I was destined to play the role of being a single parent. The first time was to my beloved son Angel Luis. His mother and I ended up divorcing when he was six years old and since then, we spent summers and Christmases together. When Angel was 12, his mother agreed to give me custody and the rest is Good-story. Suffice it to say, I tell people that when I grow up, I want to be just like my son.

Again, in 2005, and just when our daughters turned 11 years old, I became a single parent. This time it was because, as you know, my beloved wife had crossed over into the other side of Time.

At the respective Times, all three of my children were on the eve of being teenagers and I've wondered if it was just pure coincidence. Anyway, this time around I had some single-parenting experience. I continued to rely on the love I have for my children and my trust in God. Then, I did what I thought was best for them. I would talk with my daughters about staying in the Moment as long as they could and should. However, and just as important, I talked with them about staying in their *Life stage* until they grew through it.

As you know, we all go through similar stages throughout life. We start out as infants, precious bundles of joy, pure innocence and completely dependent on Mom. Then we become toddlers, crawlers, touchers, and curious about everything until we reach the age of puberty (adolescence). Then the bell sounds, "Teen!" (Teenager) and we believe we know it all, only to learn that it just seemed that way until we became adults and realized there was much more to Life than we thought we knew.

I have always heard parents talk about the "terrible twos" when referring to their toddlers and about "pre-teen" attitudes and teenage behavior. There seems to be a majority concern among parents about their children becoming Teenagers and I guess it's normal. However, as with many events in life, the first step is usually the most important. This step should determine, pace, awareness, and mental attitude. In my case, I sat down with my daughters and said the following: "Don't make a big deal about the sound of the word 'teen' in Teenager. It is just the verbal version of the number 13, placing you into a category and that is all. It is not the sounding of a bell alerting you to say and do whatever you want to do." Of course, I was being sarcastic, but I was able to capture their imagination and get my meaning across.

You see, in high school they had 15-year-old acquaintances who pretended to live the life of 21-year-olds, free from parental control and supervision and doing whatever was allowed at that age. For Teenagers, the pressure is always there because that lifestyle appears to be so exciting and enticing, perhaps even spellbinding. Regardless, they just want to fit in. It is like wanting to be a member of "the clique" and daring to eat from the Forbidden Fruit.

To help regulate that kind of pressure, I would tell my daughters, *"You don't have to be one of 'Them'. There is nothing wrong with being one of 'You'."*

So far, it appears they have chosen to heed my advice and my wisdom. They have seen what the pretenders go through. It is a fast-paced life and, too often, kids find themselves not only behind, but far off track. It's worse than trying to keep up with the Jetsons. *It is buying into a Lifestyle in which they lack the Knowledge, Experience in Time, and Wisdom necessary for coping with the reality of being a certain age.* Two of the most common consequences of this pretend lifestyle, as you know, are drug and/or alcohol abuse and teenage pregnancy. *There is a reason for "Training" wheels on bicycles.*

As they became a little older, I encouraged my daughters to *slow down* and enjoy the life they are living now. I let them know that I too was that teenager who was not 13 years old, but 13-and-a-half. I couldn't wait to be old enough to do this, that, and the other. *If I could only control the speed of Time*, I thought.

Of course, as their father, I did my part to guide them through those Times and I regularly reminded them that *even if they could live a thousand years, they would not be able to taste every fruit, forbidden or not, that the tree of Life has to offer. This is a Truth they should be mindful of as they live in Time. It is a truth that will serve them well until they run out of Life.*

As far as encouraging my children to slow down, as kids and now as young adults, I am keenly aware of just how difficult it is for them. After all, they were born as Modernity (the Beast) had shifted into high gear and had grown bigger, faster, hungrier, and more relentless than ever. For children, slowing down mean something different. Now they spend an inordinate amount of time sitting or lying around looking into a handheld screen. Going outside to play or exercise is usually not their first choice. Cuddling in modern creature comfort with their favorite tech device is just how they like it. Still, I remain hopeful. Kids today are very resourceful, intelligent, and smart. When it is time for them to take the reins of destiny, they will engage and adapt.

This is the season during which they were born and it is what they know. So there is no blame throwing here and if they were, they have company. Many young adults in their 20s, 30s, and 40s behave the same way.

For me and others born during a different Time, I was nevertheless swept up by the tsunami of Modernity, and navigating the strong and swift currents of technology took some getting used to. My daughters were born swimming in the Brackish waters where the Beast lives. I, on the other hand, found myself drifting in the same waters with currents so strong I was forced to sink or swim. I had to choose to slow down and "Be" in control if I wanted to be on my own beach. Still, it is virtually impossible to remain beached for long. The influences of the Beast are very strong and its grip just as tight. Still, for me, it is better to brave the currents than to get off the grid. Here is where regular Mindfulness tune-ups allow me to maintain my pace, catch my breath, and avoid drowning in Brackish waters.

The reality is that the Beast has made the bed we all, young and old, find comfort and convenience in, while in the midst of the constant distractions, increasing speeds and addictions. Still, making the effort to slow down is a "Good" and there is no age requirement as to when to start, you just have to want to. This suggestion loses its meaning when, to my kids, slowing down seems like swimming upstream and drifting in Brackish waters doesn't seem so bad. In fact, they are in their "unnatural" element; it is what they have always known and I understand.

I hope that I am an example to my children because they know me to be a student and practitioner of Mindfulness Meditation and they see how I am and how I live. Perhaps one day, sooner rather than later, they will realize that living in Cyberspace and at the ever increasing speeds of technology can be very stressful and that meditation can be used as a faucet to regulate the stresses they endure when they don't have to.

The bottom line is that we are all mindful to one degree or another and at one Time or another; after all, we are thinking "Beings." The perspective I have introduced throughout this book is that it is not enough to be mindful only when situations force us to be. It is to practice "Being" mindful, aware, and paying attention with intention as we are and as everything is without judgment. It is to take Time to be still, alone, and in a quiet place, just you, your breath, and your thoughts, to "Be" mindful of your own presence in the Now. Listen, there is a big difference between breathing and doing breathing exercises; being mindful and practicing Mindfulness. Start practicing.

My daughters are 21 years old now and the same "first step" advice applies. However, at this stage in Life, they have the freedom and the wisdom to choose their own paths. Their "Baby" days are behind them as well are my "Daddy" days. My daughters are young adult ladies whose father's role is now to guide, assist, and advise them, but only on an on-call basis.

You see, I am a loner, a Lone Wolf, and I have only a handful of "Friends." However, I've always encouraged my children to have friends because it is important to have relationships with other people. It is how we learn and grow as humans. Still, there are relationships and then there are "Relationships." How two people relate with each other is one of the greatest human transactions there is. It is therein the scale of human emotions reveals just who we really are in terms of overcoming and surviving beyond adversity or engendering trust and, most importantly, respect.

This brings me to the serious topic of Domestic Violence. It is a concern I have about the kind of relationships my daughters involve themselves. For me, the greatest frustration is that I cannot protect my daughters from the emotional distress of Heartbreak. At the same time, I realize that I should not have that ability. I imagine Mom might have felt differently. Still, we all have to live our own individual lives and, in our own way, learn to cope with Heartbreak and all.

Do you know anybody who has said they love their spouse, girlfriend, or boyfriend, but still abuse them? I am almost sure you do. I am sorry if you have had this unfortunate experience yourself, when words do not match behavior. I see the problem as being that *too many people use the word Love and Friend too loosely, when instead; they should tighten their relationships first. A tight relationship is based on self-respect and respect for others.*

I've always told my daughters that a solid relationship is based on a foundation of respect upon which Love is best built, not the other way around. To say you love someone, but at the same time be abusive toward them, is not at all OK. Abuse is not an expression of Love much less its engendering. There is nothing positive about it. Love, remember, is an act that incites positive feelings we identify as Love itself. Saying "I love you" is nice, but not as nice as "Being" and behaving as if you "Do." It is more about "Show" than it is about "Tell." Remember the saying, "Do unto others as you would have done unto you." Well, to abuse another, physically or otherwise, is never an act of Love and it is very important to understand why such behavior may occur. Of course, I would encourage my daughters or yours to be mindful and aware of any "red flags" that may arise and to address them immediately. It is quicker and easier to pull a weed out of the ground than it is to chop down a tree.

I believe abusers lack self-control, self-respect, and/or both, which may stem from having low self-esteem in the first place. On the other hand, the person who tolerates and accepts the abuse may also be suffering from low self-esteem. Such relationships are dysfunctional and usually lead to bad outcomes.

My daughters know that when it comes to dating, they should practice emotional control, which, as many of us know painfully well, is one of the most difficult things to do. I told them that it is Time well spent getting to know someone better before further committing. It is during this time they can show self-respect, practice self-control, and demand respect. I believe it is a good first step toward establishing clear boundaries and developing better relationships.

Starting a relationship this way, I believe, increases the probability that a strong and healthy relationship can grow and thrive with Love. Metaphorically speaking, they could otherwise find themselves in the deep end of a bad relationship before the heart begins to let go of the chokehold it has on the brain, allowing blood to flow so that the Mind can better listen and think rationally. Until then, they can find themselves drowning in depression or worse, having and acting out suicidal thoughts. The hope is that before they drown, the heart reverts to doing what it is specifically designed to do, pump blood, and the brain to do what it is designed to do, Think. I agree that this is easier said than done, but it is not impossible. Here, again, being mindful may allow thoughts to occur than can help lead one out of a bad situation.

I remind you that I am not a scientist nor do I have a PhD in anything. The advice I gave my daughters is based on my own experience, sort of a recipe, the ingredients of which are experience, trust in God, and doing the right thing for the right reasons and that it comes from the heart.

If you decide to use this recipe, you will have to make your own determination as to how much of each ingredient to use, how to use it, and under what circumstance. Otherwise, I suggest you consult a psychologist.

DRUNK WITH CHOICES

I'm going to get to a quick story about my wife, but first, here is another question: What came first, Life or Time? If you said Time, I believe you're right. I also believe that the enigma that is *"Time"* is that it is also the essence of *"Life."* Without it, we could not be born and as we are, we could not exist outside the Now, the only Time there is.

Still, we live as though we have all the Time in the world, while apparently oblivious of the Moment, oblivious of this "Now." Nevertheless, this is understandable as we are constantly exposed to so much, so fast, all the time. We find ourselves in the powerful grip of the insatiable Beast and its unrelenting influences as we live a jet-paced Life, often running late and in a hurry. This makes being mindful in the Moment, indeed very difficult. However, we must continue to try. To be aware that we "are" is the most indispensable mode to "be" in during our Journey through Life.

One of the unyielding influences of Modernity is that we are often drunk with the many, many choices we face every day and the seemingly uncontrollable impulse to choose something else. Here is an example that you're likely able to relate to.

My wife Marilyn and I were invited to a Shindig. She looked through the clothes in the closet for something to wear. Now, the closet is so full with dresses, skirts, etc.; there is little room for the few pieces of clothing that are mine. I hear my wife sigh.

"*What's wrong, babe?*" I ask.

"*I have nothing to wear,*" she says.

Then I say to her, "*Honey, you have at least 50 dresses to choose from.*"

She says, "*Yeah, but I can't decide which dress to wear.*"

So, my darling wife, after having decided that she could not choose from the clothes in the closet, gets in her car and drives miles away to a gigantic complex of stores (The Mall) where there are literally thousands of dresses to choose from. After a few hours of dress shopping, she decides that the choices are not to her liking. There is nothing there either for her to wear. So what does she do? Of course you know. She gets in her car again and drives off to another huge assemblage of stores (Another Mall), rinses, and repeats.

You know what I am talking about. Unfortunately, this is not a once in a lifetime experience; it happens all the time. *I've mentioned the speed and choice shuffle before. It is the kind of "crazy" construct of Modernity masquerading as normal.*

You will find that getting a handle on this condition is a constant challenge. However, do not allow the stress of "choosing" bring you down. Instead, *be mindful that of all the choices there will always be, there is always the choice not to choose.* So, when you have to choose, choose to be less impulsive and choose wisely. Being mindful helps; continue to at least try.

By the way, that day I had gone out to Golf with the boys and when I got home, my wife was in the closet. "*Hey honey, what did you get.*" She sighed. "*Nothing.*" "*I think I will wear the black dress I wore at your award ceremony.*" "*I remember that dress and that night.*" "*You were the most beautiful woman wearing the prettiest dress.*" She smiled and gave me a sweet kiss.

Looking back, I wonder if my wife already had that black dress in mind when she went shopping, but needed to be sure she wanted to wear it. Still, she went out into the Brackish waters where the Beast is always trolling with lures, in this case, disguised as pretty dresses and she didn't take the bait. She didn't get caught up in the "speed and choice shuffle". She chose not to choose.

FIRST THINGS FIRST IN THE PRESENT POSITIVE TENSE

When something happens that would otherwise stress me out, I simply stop in the Moment, take a deep breath, try to calm down, and focus on the "What just happened?" question. Of course, this presumes that I did not go into shock or otherwise became mentally incapacitated.

Anyway, by now, I'm alert and "Being" mindful about what just happened, and I can begin to consider what I need to do to alleviate or eliminate the problem. From this point, it is about "Doing" what first comes to mind, and in the case of an emergency, it may be the simple act of calling out to someone, 911 if need be.

The first action we take will bring us closer, take us further away, or allow the problem to persist longer than it otherwise might. Either way, at this point, it is about doing the first thing first, the second thing second, and so on and so forth until you are able to solve the problem or bring it under control. It really doesn't matter what the problem is, doing something about it is the only way to make a difference in terms of outcome and being mindful is the best mode to "Be" in. I think of this as a universal patterned response.

Anyway, as simple as it may sound, the most important thing to do before the first action is taken is actually the first thing to do and that is to "Be" fully aware of your own presence in the Moment. Being in the Moment allows you to be mindful and aware as you are and as everything "Is." From this state of "Being" and awareness, you can be informed as to what to do first, and as you do, have positive expectations about eventual outcomes.

As it is with most situations in life, it is all about "Being" aware, considering options, and then "Doing," right here, right now. It is the best time to begin to take on any problem, especially the unexpected. After all, it is happening in real Time.

Here is a quote you may want to remember if and when a negative situation arises: *"Wishing against the Present reality of a negative situation temporarily paralyzes the mind, impedes thought, and allows the onset of stress. Never wish "it" did not happen; instead, "do" something about it "Now."*

In spite of what you have just read here and in other places throughout the book, I realize that, for some of you, the idea of "Being" in the Now as you are and as everything is may not be easy, and you're right. However, it's worth a conscious and intentional effort to try to keep practicing. Throwing your hands up in the air and asking, "Why is this happening to me?" only keeps you in a bad Moment longer than you might otherwise be. This allows for the onset of stress and the delay of your arrival at what may be the next available exit (Thought) that could get you to a better place, a Mindful place, where you can "Do" sooner rather than later.

This may be the case if I were in a car accident, locked my keys in the car, had my wallet or cell phone stolen or lost, etc. On the other hand, in an altercation or dispute with someone, being "Hot Headed" only burns positive thoughts that may otherwise occur to you, causing you instead to miss the entrance, ("Being" mindful) the result of which may very well lead to the commission of actions that may be regrettable, perhaps for the rest of your life.

For these and many other reasons, making the conscious effort to be mindful in the Now, as you are and as everything is without judgment may be critically important. It is where you want to "Be." It is the best place to "Be." It is from this "Place," a "Mindful" place, where the kinds of thoughts are likely to occur, increasing the probability of being successful in moving beyond your present situation. It is from a Mindful place where you come to terms with the fact that your Present reality is not your Future reality; it can't be. The Present and the Future are mutually exclusive Times and cannot occupy the same Instant. It is only because there are separated by an Instant that they seem seamless. Nevertheless, that same Instant may be all the Time we need for the right thought to occur. This awareness is what I think of as a kind of "balance" more likely achievable with regular Mindfulness practice.

Remember, everything is happening in the "Now" and it is the only Time we can do something about almost anything. It is time to start to do or to continue to do those things that can make your life just a little better. Try to not let your thoughts wander outside of the "Now" as they will, and when they do, let them slide by and gently come back to the thoughts about what you need to or should be doing in the moment. When we allow ourselves to be distracted by thoughts of helplessness, it makes it more difficult to move beyond a bad moment. It makes it difficult to maintain balance.

However, shifting thoughts is not necessarily a bad thing. If your thoughts shift to the past for reference, it could be helpful. Drawing from similar experience to help us cope with a present reality can only help. On the other hand, if the challenge is new and we have no reference, "Being" in the moment as you are and as everything is, is still the best place to "Be" if the best thoughts are to occur.

But, are we truly ever without reference? I don't believe so. Consciously or subconsciously, I believe there is always reference.

Think about it, where do Thoughts come from? "From my mind, from my thinking," you say. This still does not answer the question. Here is another question: Do we really need to know where thoughts come from? I don't think so. Instead, I use my energy acting on thoughts as they occur to me.

There is a basic economic postulate that states: *everything in Life relates to everything else in Life*. I understand this to mean that everything we experience and every thought associated with any experience and even thoughts yet to occur to us are all within the realm of the human experience. It is when we are "Being" mindful as we are and as everything is without judgment that the best thoughts are likely to occur. In my life, this has been my experience.

It also helps me to be mindful that a challenge is but one of many experiences during my entire life and that I am *always* living my entire life right here, right now. I am mindful that *there is nothing more powerful and positive than the present moment. Yes, Life itself is powerful and positive and Time and Thoughts provide the driving force that transports us into the future*.

Fortunately, for most of us, difficult or unexpected challenges, bad news, and bad things are the exception. What is more fortunate is that good news and good things are usually more prevalent in our daily lives.

For me, as a Mindfulness Meditation practitioner, I've found it easier to move beyond the bad Times and as well perceptively stay in the Present Positive Tense a moment or two longer during the good Times. Being mindful and accepting what "is," is where I want to be when the good times are here or when I am faced with challenges, challenges I will continue to face until I run out of Life—so too will you.

Too often and for too many, the present negative tense is where we usually find ourselves, and too often, we find ourselves stuck there for too long. When I say long, I am talking about seconds to minutes long, and unfortunately, for too many, hours to days long on end. *I believe that staying in the Present Negative Tense for too long rots the Spirit.*

It can make a big difference in your life the amount of Time you stay in the Present Negative Tense or Present Positive Tense. Life happens and sometimes we have little or no control when it does. However, we have a degree of control over the thoughts we have about those events and if we are not aware that we do, events may persist. Of course, if the event is negative, the sooner we begin to focus on positive thoughts as they relate to solving our problems or accepting the inevitable, the sooner the right thought may occur, the sooner we are able to regulate our emotions and move on. With a positive mindset, we are more likely to survive our challenges and continue to grow well.

On the better side of Life, when good things happen, *the longer we are mindful about staying in the Present Positive Tense, the longer the good Times seem to roll.* Now keep in mind that we live in instances of Time and, as such, the bad times and the good times happen in increments of Time shorter than the instance we live in.

The good news is that the instances of the "bad" or the "good" do not constitute the "ongoing" of your entire life; *they are simply temporary fragments.*

I hope this idea is not too simple to grasp because it could be. I've been asked if I was playing mind games when I talk about Life in Time in this way, and I'm not. If you believe I am, *I hope you win.* It is simply my point of view, my own thinking. It is what occurs to me and I can only hope I am being helpful enough for you to indulge me.

We live day by day, as they say, but with a lazy urgency that we will get over and beyond whatever it is that stresses us. Some choose simply to ignore, and it is true, some problems just seem to disappear. Maybe this proves the point I have been making: *"Life lasts but an instant."*

I remember the late Earl Nightingale saying that 80% of the things we worry about do not come to pass. Regardless of the percentages, in my life, this has been true more times than not. How about you?

We have all said it at one time or another: "Time really flies." "It seems like it was just yesterday." Well, ask yourself, why would something that happened years ago seem like it had happened just yesterday? I'll tell you why. I believe this is so simply because everything you have experienced in life so far amounts to who you are in this Instant, this Moment, this Now as you live your Entire life. Still, the reality is that Time "*is*" and has always been a constant element and there is but only one Time and that time is "Now." Just the same, and what we can be sure about, is that our entire life always equal "Now."

You've heard the phrase, "This too shall pass." Perhaps this kind of thinking is why we live as though we have a thousand years to fix whatever is going on in our lives. It is as though we intentionally ignore the truth about our reality, Time, and our mortality. Of course, everything will pass. *Time makes sure of it.*

Finish the following statement: "If it ain't broke…" I knew you would fall for it. Think of it this way: "*If it ain't broke, don't break it; leave it alone.*" There are, and will always be, situations in our lives that we cannot fix and others we should not even try to fix. We cannot bring a loved one back to Life after Death or stop acts of Nature. Then, one day, it dawns on us that Time is spending us out of Life. It is like gaining weight or like watching grass grow: seemingly, all of a sudden, our clothes fit tightly and we need to lose weight; the grass blades are long and need mowing. Seemingly, all of a sudden, we are 40, 60, or 80 years old. Panic sets in and it seems we are running out of Time. For older folks, the watch and the calendar now have their attention on a regular basis. Birthdays are sour-sweet and celebrated with some degree of anxiety. "There is nothing to see here, it's just Life happening, keep moving." Still, slow down, pay attention, and be Mindful; a Lifetime is just that. We are born, we live, and then we run out of Life. We do not run out of Time; we simply die. *A lifetime could be one Moment long or 100 years of Moments long. Yes, we live one moment at a time, in one continuous "Now."*

Being constantly distracted as we usually are, it is easy to see why it seems we subconsciously ignore the passing of Time as it relates to the end of Life, and perhaps it is unnatural to always be so mindful. Still, there is nothing going on in the past or in the future and I can only account for "Now," the only Time I live. Still, there is no way to know just how long we have before Time spends us out of Life.

Nevertheless, we seem to live oblivious to the reality that as Time elapses, so does Life, and it is understandable. In the Constance of Time, life is an incremental experience.

I say this to draw attention to the need we have for each other in order to make sense of Time. It is necessary for our survival as a species, especially in a modern world. Even so, do we really need to understand Time, perhaps? Regardless however, we have to accept that *"Time" just "is," and there is nothing we can do about it.* A better approach to Time would be to focus our efforts and energies as we *strive always to understand Life and our own separate and individual "Being" as we live relative to the Present Living Moment as opposed to understanding Time. Remember, we are all incidental to Time.*

Ironically, we talk about spending Time, even though the reality is that *Time is the only thing that does the spending. In fact, Reality shows us that Time spends us all into "Nothingness" or into "Something" we know nothing about.*

I've said it before. As we are born, we simultaneously begin to die as Time travels on. It's just what Time does. *We are ushered into the world as Time's guests; we stay for a while and then we leave when Time checks us out.*

Here is another way to look at it with a question you should consider answering. *We come into this world through a gate in Time and we live until we run out of Life exiting through another gate and into the other side of Time. Where that gate leads to may very well depend on what you really believe.* Now, what do you believe?

Meanwhile, our lives are spent as the sands in the hourglass of our lives trickle through with the passage of Time. There are no refunds or discounts. You can't get yesterday back and you can't get extra Time today. Paradoxically, we don't get Time; we're born in it.

This is why, in the urgency of the moment, we should be living Now, fully aware and being mindful that we always live and die in the present, when we should be living in the Present Positive Tense, thinking Now, thinking Positive.

CONNOISSEURS OF SENSATION AND EMOTION

It just occurred to me to ask you the following questions. Can you "feel" old? "Of course, I can," you say. However, how do you know what "old" feels like if you are not "old"? If you are "old," do everything about you and your life feel "old," of course not? Are feelings older people experience perceived or real? For that matter, are feelings anyone feel real or perceived? Answers to these questions may seem obvious. What is not as obvious, however, is that because we can only exist in the Present, it is the only Time we experience "Being" as we are and as we live our entire lives in the Now, lives that last but an Instant.

The question then is, who is old or who is young based on how anyone can and does feel in the Present Living Moment, in this Instant. Perhaps it's just an individual thing, your thing.

I think of it as there being two "olds," the psychological and the physical. The physical "old," though obvious, will vary from person to person and any variance may be attributable to lifestyle, disease, or DNA. Naturally, older people wear the suffrage of physical decline from the abrasive passage of Time. Seventy-year-old bodies naturally carry 70-year-old skin, kidneys, hearts, lungs, and a 70-year-old skeletal structure that supports them.

In a modern world where there are available means by which we can literally transfigure our bodies, many avail themselves. Still, you can dress up a 70-year-old person with the latest fashion, plastic surgery, implants, Botox and makeup, but the person remains 70 years old.

Nevertheless, looking old and feeling old are two different experiences. The feeling of joint pain, for example, is not necessarily an age attributing experience even though it is usually a late age condition.

I remember feeling knee pain when I was 17 years old and it may have been because of the many miles I ran and the thousands of kicks I practiced when I trained for tournaments. This is also true today of many young, strong, and healthy professional athletes.

Listen, I understand and accept that all things being equal and natural over Time, these kinds of conditions are likely to affect older folks and that those who still to this day jog, ride bikes, and play tennis are the exception to the rule. Then there are, as I described, exceptions made possible because of advances in science and medicine.

My focus here though is on the Present moment and how we are feeling. If you are feeling good now, it is because you are feeling good now, and that's that. The key here is to be mindful that you are feeling what you are feeling while you are "feeling." Because, it is important to notice; otherwise, you will miss the Present moment and not be able to appreciate the feeling and the meaning it gives your life while it lasts. As you know, this is what we call, in many different situations, "taking something for granted until we find ourselves losing it or having lost it." If you don't "notice" something, you will simply miss it. Try to be mindful about reminding yourself to slow down and savor your "Being" in the instance of your life, your entire life.

So just how important is it to miss the present Moment, very? It is important because your life may depend on it; when we miss the Present, we never get a second chance at it because it's gone forever. This usually happens when we are distracted by thoughts about Times outside the Now. When this happens, we lose our sense of Presence and the opportunity to fully appreciate all that is happening in the Moment. This, of course, includes how we are feeling.

Regardless of age, however, we feel how we are feeling now, and nothing else should matter except being aware and mindful as we enjoy the good moments, as we immerse our "Self" in them.

On the other hand, we are most mindful when what we are feeling is hurtful or unpleasant. It is when our sensitivity is highest. Every moment, every instant we're adversely affected, is an instant or moment too long and we are forced to be mindful; we can't help but notice. Still, good, bad, or unpleasant, how we feel is our present reality, and whether we are forced or being intentional, being mindful makes a difference.

Mindfulness allows me to acknowledge my feelings for what they are. I find that when I embrace my feelings, perceived or real, I am better able to regulate them. Fortunately, most of the time, we feel good or, at worst, not bad, and it's OK.

So, who is to say that the pain felt by younger people is more or less than the pain the 70-year-old feels? I believe pain is pain. *Exactly what that feels like may very well depend on one's reference, perception, level of tolerance, and/or ability to regulate how we feel.*

As far as being psychologically old, Life is mostly about our emotional "Being." I am sure you've heard the quote, "It's not how old you are, but how young you feel" and there is nothing wrong with expressing yourself in the Present Positive Tense. Still, let's be honest here. This is something older people say to mitigate the reality of being a certain age, and this too is OK. We are who we are; however, there is a suggestion that there are "old" emotions as compared "young" emotions.

So, let's see how this sounds, "I feel happy in an older way." It doesn't even sound right, does it? "Because I am 70 years old, my love for you is a 70-year-old love." This too is as ridiculous as it sounds. So, who determines what "old" feels like? You do, of course. It's personal; it's your own experience.

Take these two people for example: one is 17 years old and the other 73. Is it possible that both can experience the same feeling or emotion and recognize it as such? I believe so. If a 73-year-old person said that he/she felt good, healthy, and happy, are those feelings 73 years old as well? I don't believe so. I believe that feelings and emotions do not have an age, and every one of us experiences what we feel in our own way. Furthermore, we describe how we feel based on our own individual reference and Mindfulness at the time; not our age.

Therefore, the 17-year-old cannot say that she/he feel better, or happier, or healthier than the 73-year-old. Moreover, the 73-year-old person may actually feel better, or at least have, in "Being" mindful, a greater appreciation for the feeling. *After all, he/she have had 73 years of Sensation and Emotion experience.*

Here is a story about what I mean. It is a story about love. I know a woman who worked in the mayor's office a few years ago. At this moment, I do not recall her name, but the name Marilyn comes to mind. Anyway, Marilyn was sweetly pleasant, yet reserved, and she always dressed elegantly—a classy Lady who kept herself well. *I would think to myself that she had to have been a knockout when she was young.*

Anyway, I believe she was about 55 years old at the time and was widowed. One day, I visited her office and found her to be unusually cheerful. Her eyes sparkled and she spoke with her smile. I asked her, "What, today, are you so happy about?" She whispered to me that she had met an ex-boyfriend from way back in high school and that he too was widowed. I spent a few moments with her to listen to her story. I got the full scoop, wished her all the best with her reunion, and left.

About three weeks later, I visited her office and she was as giddy as a schoolgirl with a crush on the most popular boy on campus. She had been going out on dinner dates with the man. I was so happy for her and so was everyone else in her office. She had been floating on a "Happy Cloud" for months before she announced that the man had proposed to marry her.

At first, I thought, "That was fast." Today I know better. Love never comes too late or too early, and my friend had fallen and was "Being" in love NOW and that was all that mattered. She was "Being" happy.

These two people came together as destiny would have them, and at a "Now" in which their entire lives became one of Love and Happiness. Age had nothing to do with it, nor did it matter.

So, as you can see, my lady friend, the gentleman, and the 73-year-old man at their respective ages and with so much *"Emotion and Sensation experience" can be considered Connoisseurs or Knowers of the Self.* With so many years of experience in "Being" and "Feeling," I think this is a title well deserved.

Furthermore, from the many years of experience older folks have lived through, they have the kind of wisdom younger people, especially their children, rely on. For older folks, this kind of wisdom includes lessons learned from experiences lived over Time, a 20/20 vision once viewed through the lens of hindsight. However, let's agree there is no great secret here. It is what Time does. On the descent from the mountain of Life, there is little reliance on hindsight, but lots of wisdom to share.

Nevertheless, there is no point in lamenting that, "If I knew then what I know now," I would have made a very different decision. I would have invested. I would have stayed with that person."

In retrospect, we would have done a thousand things differently, but we didn't. Such lamentations are at the expense of the Present Living Moment when we could be making new choices as we experience our continuous "Being" and "Becoming" of ourselves. Being mindful as you are and as everything is without judgment is usually the best place to be in terms of moving forward with meaning and purpose, so move on.

Don't be hard on yourself, however. I'm almost sure that most of the decisions you have made to date have been good ones and that your life, for the most part, "Is" actually good.

Remember that Life and "Being" alive are mostly sensational and emotional experiences that can only have meaning in the Now, meaning only you can experience.

Also, and as often as you can, be mindful that the emotions we describe as Love, Hate, Sadness, and Happiness and sensations of Pain and Pleasure are as ageless as Time. It is all about experiencing your own Presence in the moment and "Being" mindful that, in it, we live our entire lives, right here, right now, and that *Life lasts but an Instant.*

ALL WE'LL NEED

I think it's a good idea to take stock of what "Things" we now have in our lives and in our homes. We should rethink their cost in terms of the stress it took to acquire these things and the stress we endure to keep them. What we don't have to clean on a regular basis, we have to repair, replace, or maintain. Then, one day, we look around only to find our homes cluttered with stuff that should be outright disposed of or put away in storage. But it's OK; we can build, buy, or rent storage space, right? Think about it: We buy a beautiful house, make a home of it, and then we proceed to fill it up with "Stuff." It may take a few years before we realize that there is stuff we have not seen or used for at least a year, and then, what do we do, you know it: "garage sale!"

But what's the point of having a garage sale, you're right again, to make room for new stuff? What about the people who buy your stuff? Of course, they fill their homes with it. It's a stuff accumulation and transfer cycle, the kind of activity and behavior that is a part of our culture. By the way, the stuff we buy from garage sales look like stolen goods neatly placed in our homes.

Seriously, though, getting rid of stuff and creating space in our homes makes for a lighter ambiance. With the extra space, there is more oxygen in the rooms, and it feels easier to breathe. I don't know about you, but it's like clearing out and cleaning my car. The air inside is conditioned, it smells good and it runs a lot smoother and faster. Yeah, I know, it only seems that way. Still, it is my own perception and it feels good.

Anyway, the message here again is that our entire lives equal this One Present Moment. Therefore, we should take care to fill our lives with what's most important: Love and Companionship, not Things.

By the way, some of us don't have the time or inclination to have a garage sale. Instead, we donate to the Salvation Army. It's for a good cause and it is easy. Give them a call and they will come and pick up your "Stuff" and give you a receipt you may use for tax purposes.

I digress. Realize that when we were infants and at the beginning of our journey through Life, *all we needed was Love and Care.* The same is true when we are old and on the last few miles of our journey; again, *all we will need is Love and Care.*

Fortunately, for us as Humans, Love and Care are almost as ageless as Time itself. It never gets old to love and care for others and for others to love and care for us. From the moment we are born, we are welcomed into the world with love and in caring arms without which we could not survive. It is when the "Welcoming" party starts and we embark upon our own Journey through life. Then, when we are in the waning stretch of our journey, we become as vulnerable as we were when we were infants and needing love and care. However, now the kind of love and care has a different purpose and meaning. It is now to provide comfort and companionship given with love, care, and now, with compassion as we are ushered into the other side of Time, the same Time it was when our journey began: Now O'clock.

During the Time between our entry and our departure, here and now; where is all that love and care to be found? I ask the question because too often we are not mindful to be loving and caring when we could be. I try to be, as often as I can, and it's not easy. Being mindful requires an awareness of our own "Being" in our own presence amidst the constant barrage of distractions and the Mind-bending speeds of modernity. This makes it almost impossible to always be able to behave with care and love, even when the opportunities are available to us and it's OK. Those of us who try to be so mindful, will love and care more often than most do. When I say, "It is OK," I do so while being aware of the reality that there are so many aspects to our lives and that in any given moment, loving and caring may not be the only Present concern. Another concern may be accountability or self-preservation. Remember, it is best to "Be" in a position of strength and awareness if we are to "Do," to love, to care for someone else.

Meanwhile, we should as often and as long as we can, with awareness, ignore the constant distractions that can cause us to miss *the Present Moment, the only Time we can share Love and Care with each other*. Sadly, enough, those missed moments are lost forever and this loss is a very high price to pay for living past each other without loving and caring, or just being human for goodness' sake. Now, "Being" mindful, reflect on this for a moment.

LIFE AND DEATH

We should all try to slow down to a speed, mentally and/or physically, that allows us to be mindful of our own presence in the Now. We need not ignore the obvious, that all our experiences can only happen in the Present. It is always a good idea to, as often as you can, practice "Being" aware of your own presence. I say this because the ever-increasing speeds and the constant distractions of a modern lifestyle make it so that our sense of presence escapes us more often than we realize.

Knowing this, it is up to us to make an honest effort to pay attention with intention, to "Being" here and now, as Life happens. It makes no difference whether we are having a good experience or a bad one. The reality is that our *entire* life is a temporary experience in terms of Time. So, as I said before, any experience, negative or positive, in our lives is even more temporary more times than not. *Death is the only and ultimate exception. Our experiences do not survive us. When we run out of life (die), they end.*

Unfortunately, too many people live their lives with a conscious or subconscious fear of death. Ironically, some have their own special preference about how and when they would like to die. Some say they want to live to see the day when— (fill in the blank). Others say they want to die in their sleep. Still others say they don't want to die before— (fill in the blank). Then there are those who even have plans for death and beyond. Now, I'm not talking about going to heaven. I'm talking about those who want their bodies flash-frozen after death with the hope that someday in the future, advancements in science and medicine will make their resuscitation possible. The scientific name for this is Cryonics.

In our modern world, Death has become a multibillion-dollar industry and it has a Life of its own. Morgues, funeral parlors, psychologists, insurance companies, and others thrive financially. It's the business of Death and we all find some benefit, some convenience, some consolation, and some acceptance because of the service the Death industry provides.

But why fear Death? It is futile and irrational to fear this inevitable phase of life; yes, I said *phase*. Still, I realize that it may simply be that we came to know Life and that Death is the inevitable passage to an unknowable eternity. Regardless, I think of Death as simply a transition into the other side of Time and not as a way to allay a fear I might have. Instead what I am, is curious as to what's next. Furthermore, I believe that the fear others have may be just an "anxious" curiosity about the "transition" and not a fear of Death itself—think about it.

Meanwhile, as I live, I do not think of Death as a Foe. I live believing that *"Death" too, may very well be my last best friend*. I live with the confidence that my best friend will be there to usher me through my transition into the other side of Time.

As far as the "Death" industry is concerned, well, it will continue to exist so long as there is a birth rate, so long as there is a human pulse.

Still, and even though we all know that death is inevitable, too many of us drive through life with one foot on the gas pedal and the other foot on the brake. In case you do not realize it, people who are safety conscious die too, and people who live recklessly outlive them a lot of the time.

For many, just the thought of Death can be a bit scary, and the unknown usually is. Fortunately for those of you who trust God and believe in Heaven, you have nothing to lose and Glory to gain. Those of you should "Be" free to lift your foot off the brakes more often and for a moment longer. I am willing to bet you are not going to run out of Life any sooner.

Here is a thought: *"Be" open to Life and do not let the fear of Death close your "Living" door.* Know that the fear of Death is merely a thought we can only entertain in the Present Living Moment. It is an anxiety we have about the future that may be at the expense of the Now if we let it. Think about this: As far as the past is concerned, we cheat Death every morning when we wake up, every breath we take and every moment that passes as Time elapses and until we run out of Life. My curious and sometimes suspicious mind thinks of this as some sort of Russian roulette where the mystery player, in this game (Life) designed by God, may very well be my last best friend.

Until the game is played out, it is a new day, but being awake is not enough. We should use the present wakeful Moment to turn on our minds, take the first full breath of the day, and "Be" fully aware and mindful as we are and as everything *is* in the Present Positive Tense. Always expect that something good will happen today, to you or to someone you love.

Regardless of whatever is happening in our lives, we should at least try to live positively, passionately and fearlessly. We should let more people and ideas into our lives. We should do something we have never done before or at least do something we have not done in a long time. It could be something as simple as finding your way to a place where you can see a sunset or a sunrise. Maybe, you can get a telescope and star gaze at night. How about sky diving? I dare you. Whatever you have in mind, you can only "Do" on this side of Time. Think of it as spicing up your life as you have it, here and now; you may as well.

Either way, at some point in Time, perhaps when you least expect it, you are going to run out of Life as Time continues to carry those who survive you into the future. Put another way: at any given "Now," *we are all perfect and timely candidates for Death and as far as Death is concerned, we are all exactly the same and precise age: "Now" old.*

The last thing I have to say about death is that the sooner you take control over the fear of running out of Life (dying), or better yet, change your perspective, the sooner you will realize a more fun, positive, purposeful, and fulfilling Life. Challenge Death—not by living recklessly but by living mindfully, hopefully, purposefully, passionately, and fearlessly. You don't have to carry the weight of the fear of Death on your back as you Journey through life. You want to be light on your feet as you stand in your door and face the Sun, and if it crosses your mind, think of Death as just a shadow behind you. Step outside with the lack of care or concern Death deserves. Expect that something good is going to happen to you today. Why not? You have life now. Embrace it; breathe it in, Live it.

DOING

When I think about "Being" and all there is to "Do" or to say about "Now," I'm overwhelmed, and it is simply because, as we live our entire lives right here, right now, it is impossible to do it all. Time will not allow because "Now" is constantly elapsing as the finite nature of Life simultaneously extinguishes as it ignites. This in itself is one of Life's most powerful and intriguing paradoxes. It is to say that *we live our entire lives in a span of an instant, yet a lifetime is not enough time to do it all.* There is just so much "Doing" to do and the passage of Time will simply not allow it without an opportunity cost. In other words, *we could "Talk" about Life now or "Do" something with Life now.*

"Doing" is powerful; however, in real Time, nothing happens without first "Being" and being fully aware and mindful as you are and as everything is without judgment makes it essential to get the most out of what you do with Life "Now."

Regrettably, having to "Do" in a hurry, (keeping up with the Jetsons) robs us of the true value of Life in the Present Living Moment, when at best we can only get a glance of it, a glance of the instance of our lives. This usually happens when we behave as if we can live faster than the speed of Now. Again, what's the point of going on a sightseeing tour on a bus that's moving at 150 mph?

Furthermore, continuing to allow ourselves to drift in the strong and rapid currents of a Modernity that offers quantity and not necessarily quality, we keep missing the exit to a better life, a life that is ours to choose.

Listen, if you want a quality Life, and you should, you will just have to make up your Mind to slow down and choose how and when to take your own exit into that Life. You're going to have to be the bacon in a "bacon and egg" breakfast.

The "when" is obvious, "Now," the ONLY Time you can do something about almost anything. The "how," as I continue to suggest, is through "Being" mindful about the choices you make, starting with slowing down so that as you approach your own exit you can actually take it and not miss it again. Everything else will fall in place as you continue to "Be" mindful as you live your entire Life moving forward.

For those who would like the world to stop so they can jump off, remember that "Control" is there for those who choose to take it. The idea of jumping off, as a metaphor is rather extreme, and as such, would certainly be a permanent solution to what is likely a temporary and manageable situation. Of course, there are those for whom the metaphor may be a real contemplation and so may be in need of therapy. However, in too many cases, it is not that there are no choices or that we ran out of choices. Instead, it is that we run out of ideas perhaps due to "impossibility thinking" or that we lose the Will, the Will to choose another course of action, another way to live.

One way to choose a course of action, regardless of the situation, I believe, is to first stop in the moment and "Be" mindful about what is happening and accepting it for what it is without judging it. *"Being" as you are makes it easier for you to pay attention to what it is you're experiencing. This moment of Mindfulness may be all the Time you need for the best thoughts to occur, allowing for a better, or at least a different course of action.*

On the "better" hand, slowing down and "Being" mindful perceptively gives you a second or two longer to enjoy your moment if what you are experiencing are good Times. Think of it as stretching your present living moments for just a few instances longer. For me, sometimes it seems like I'm seeing my life unfold one frame at a time and I like that.

When it is all said and done, and from beginning to end, Life is about making choices, especially those choices readily available that can make a positive difference in how we experience "Being" happy in the unfolding Present Living Moments of our lives.

We're all aware that it is impossible to actually live faster than the speed of "Now." Regardless, however, this does not stop us from impulsively racing through Life at the expense of the Moment, an expense we incur by our seemingly uncontrollable tendency to "Thought Surf," Channel Surf, or Web surf. What's insane is that, often, we do all three at the same time. It's like casting a net and capturing a million bits of information, like puzzle pieces that do not fit to create a clear and specific image of our own "Being" in the Now. There is no focus, no paying attention; there is only the blur of information overload. Mind mud, I call it.

As a reminder, this is what to expect when trying to keep up with the Jetsons in a modern world with ever increasing speeds, more powerful and insidious influences, stronger addictions, and an increasing array of constant distractions. This is what to expect when we spend an inordinate amount of Time on some planet in cyberspace.

Fortunately, we need not be stranded or lost in cyberspace. We can steer our Mindful ship off and away, and "Now" is always a good Time to take command and control and exit the Jet race we find ourselves in every day. It is your choice how you want to live in the belly of the Beast. You just have to make up your mind to choose.

Remember, we cannot eliminate the Beast, nor is it necessary to do so. However, what we can do is, from Time to Time, "fast" from its milk. We certainly can do without the G-Force (Go-Force) that stresses us out when we are not in control.

By now I hope that you have, at least, started thinking about slowing down and about how Mindfulness can help you; not to change anything, but in seeing reality for what it is and not what you wish it to be. Here I remind you that to perceive reality however you do, is only an exercise in your own mind. It does not change reality for what it "is." Life is real and it happens as it does in real time. Mindful of this, I believe better choices are made and difficult ones are made easier.

As you have been reading all along, you know I am convinced that the volitional ability to slow down is best accomplished through the knowledge and practice of Mindfulness Meditation on a regular basis. In fact, if you are to practice, you will first have to do more than slow down: you are required to be still, just you, your breath, and your thoughts for the duration of your session. As you will see, you can slow down; you just have to want to.

For me, regular Mindfulness practice has not only opened doors in my Mind, but has also opened my Mind to recognize the doors I should leave closed. For example, some things are better left unsaid and sometimes it is better not to go "there."

You know, after the first publication of Now O'clock, it always needled me that I could make it a better and more beneficial read, but I was just being lazy. It was not until I discovered Mindfulness Meditation and became a regular practitioner that I gained a better sense of my own "Being." It was the kind of awareness that inspired me to redirect my life, to write and publish this revision. Otherwise, I would not have. I had already decided it was too much work and I was lazy. Of course now I am glad I did and I hope you are too.

Practicing has and continues to make a real positive and more meaningful difference in my daily Life and in my relationship with my children, my fellow people, and especially, my Self. There is nothing like being aware and mindful of my own "Being" in the Present, in the Now, Mind, Body and Soul, in the occasion of my entire Life. You too, may find meaning and great health benefits in appreciating the "Instance" of your Life by "Being" mindful, slowing down, and taking control. Fortunately for each of us, whatever benefits derived only need be described in our own individual way as they manifest in our lives and as we experience and enjoy them in the Present Positive Tense. Remember, you are the only "You" there ever was or will ever be. So, whatever the experience, it is always all yours; it is always all mine, it is never ours. However, it is always ours to share and we should.

Perhaps most importantly, we should not ignore that there is a difference between being alive and living. Being alive has nothing to do with whether it is nine o'clock in the afternoon, Friday morning, or your birthday. We are alive simply because we are; we're alive only because we breathe.

On the other hand, most of the "living" we do is without concern for what time it is or what day it is even though we don't realize we're unconcerned. Sometimes not thinking about something is easier than thinking about it, but it is when we really don't have to think that we drift. This is when the cunning and insatiable Beast choreographs our routine.

It is important that our focus be on "Being" aware that *living is a "doing" proposition fueled by emotions and steered by our thoughts.* Of course, if we are to take control, we must first "Be" so that we may "Do" in terms of choosing how we want to live while in the belly of the Beast. Being able to recognize its influences makes it easier to resist them, and resist them we should because the Ads that keep calling you back again and again for the latest fix will not stop running. Time is the currency required to keep those Ads running and the Beast has nothing but Time on its side. On the other hand, for you and me, the exhaustible nature of Life is usually announced in the one Ad we will never live to read; our obituary.

We have in many ways become conditioned and very accustomed to living within the constructs designed by Modernity (The Beast) and so much so that choosing to live off the "Grid" may be a stress we could not endure for too long. A better course of action is choosing to disconnect from Time to Time as a way to manage the stress of living in the belly of the Beast. Of course, it all starts with "Being" in control. Suffice it to say, I once saw a picture of a beautiful rose growing out of a pile of garbage. Just the same, you can design a beautiful life even while living in the belly of the Beast. You just have to choose it.

Nevertheless, after all is said and done, I cannot say that a man lying on the deck of his yacht sipping on a Mimosa somewhere in the Caribbean is happier than the Yanomamo hunter in the Amazon rainforest sitting around a fire eating a Tapir (pig) he killed that day. They both are living the experience of a true emotion of happiness in their own way and in their own circumstance. The Mimosa is a modern concoction while the Tapir is a natural offering of the forest caught in traps set by the Yanomamo. Unlike the Tapir, we, the "modern man," are conditioned to be caught in the many traps set for us by the Beast. But, it does not always have to be that way. We can avoid many of the traps when we choose to "Be" mindful, and in control.

Listen, Life is about "Being" naturally happy, and all things being equal, he/she who is truly happy with what amounts to very little, is indeed successful at Life. Still, one can be happy in the belly of the Beast so long as it is a life they have chosen and not one constructed for them by the Beast itself. Of course, to be able to choose, again, one must first be mindful and in control.

Remember, everything relates to everything else in life, and so I can only hope that something you've read in this book sparks your interest and stains your memory and that you may ponder its meaning. It may be a question asked, a question you answered, a Quote or a Thought. If you find that you are inspired and moved to change your life, perhaps you should write about it. In fact, I strongly encourage you to do so.

"*Life lasts but an instant*" was such a thought for me and having pondered its meaning brought me here the first time. Now, this revision was inspired by the realization that there is a seamless link between Time and Life and Life and Mindfulness. Its added perspective, I hope, has made Now O'clock, a more meaningful and beneficial read for you.

Now, having practiced Mindfulness on a regular basis has helped me to find my own pace, and among everything else, I am also more mindful of my senses. Now, the foods I eat and what I drink taste the way they are supposed to taste. Think about it, chewing what you eat for just a moment longer and letting what you drink bathe your tongue will make for a more palatable and delightful experience. On the other hand, and what too many are in the bad habit of doing, eating on the run, is nothing more than putting food in your mouth and making it disappear. Guilty?

Look, I realize many of us have only one hour for lunch and dinnertime can be just as hurried, but this is not a good reason to behave that way. Unfortunately, too many people use Time as an excuse and this is why it is so important to slow down. When we are mindful to eat less and really take time to taste our meal as we eat it, we will find that an hour is more than enough time. Your meal will taste better, and your "eating" experience will be more satisfying. You will never feel stuffed again and you may actually lose weight because you will be eating less. Don't worry; you will not starve to death.

Staying in the Instance of your life a second or two longer allows us to take a closer look and to listen more attentively. Here again, "being "mindful makes clear the differences between looking as opposed to just seeing and listening as opposed to just hearing. I would not have to ask you if you heard me if you were listening. I would not have to ask you if you saw if you were looking. Things like coffee, bread, and roses smell better and the texture of your life improves.

"Being" mindful, we become more productive at whatever we do. The things we do are much more valuable, much more human, and much more memorable. Relationships with your spouse, your parents, family, and friends will always make for special occasions even on ordinary days. There would be more celebrating Life just because it is "Now." Life becomes simply better, more meaningful and happier.

Remember, keeping your dream alive in your mind while in its pursuit will always be better than not having a dream to keep alive. The anxious anticipation keeps you lively as and until your dream becomes your Present Living Reality. Meanwhile, taking care of something, or especially someone, is better than not caring for nothing or no one.

Be aware that your entire life is, at all times, happening within and around you. The people around you, loved ones, friends, and family that are part of your life and may or may not be directly involved, are sources of inspiration that can help you keep your enthusiasm gas tank full so that you may cross the last mile toward your future Present Living Reality—your Dream come true.

They may be the same people who would, either way, be there in the event that Life happened in a way so your dream did not come true. They may be the greatest source of support when you most need them to be. Who knows, if you continue to swim in the same stream of consciousness, if you continue to be mindful, born may yet be a new idea in the cradle of your mind, a new idea to care for, a new dream to keep alive.

Remember, *nothing scares away "failure" more than another "try" and that nothing is more attractive to "success" than courage. Better a Life on a journey experiencing success with anxious anticipation than a Life parked on the side of any road.*

Remind yourself, your children, and those you care for, there never was, there is not, and there never will be anyone better that you at "Being" You. You are already the best and are always becoming more of who you are, as you are never the same "You" twice.

Furthermore, and as you are, stay open to Life and don't let the fear of "Death" close your "Living" door. Confidently walk through your door every day and into the Life you choose to live. I say this because too often we think of "Death" as a worst-case scenario, when instead, we should think of "Death" as, maybe, our last best friend. Paradoxically, we think of Time as being a limited resource available to us when, in reality, it is Life that is finite. In other words, when we think that we're running out of Time, what is actually happening is that we are running out of Life; we die, pure and simple. We should not live in fear of our last best friend, whose visit with us is inevitable. Soon enough we will be in his embrace as he ushers us into the other side of Time.

Again, we come into this world through a gate in Time and we live until we run out of Life, exiting through another gate and into the other side of Time. Where that gate leads to may very well depend on what you really believe. Again, ask yourself, "What do I really believe"?

Meanwhile, always expect that something good will happen to you today and if it doesn't and nothing bad happened, then it was a good day, a day to be grateful.

Still, believe in miracles and in God's blessings upon us on this side of Time, blessings that are answers to prayers made or not made and which purpose is more important than form. Trust God, and as you do your best, be patient and trust your destiny.

At this point, right here, right now, whatever you are thinking about doing, or have been thinking about for a long time before Now, do it now if it's available to you. Promise yourself to start, continue, or stop doing something; begin a new life. Learn about and start practicing Mindfulness. Don't quit on an idea you have been working on or make the first step into the mile toward a new goal. Remember, while Success is a series of emotional experience lived while in pursuit of a worthy goal, the achievement of that goal never arrives too late if you still have life and the mindful ability to appreciate what is happening in your life at the time.

Difficult as it may be, if you are living a self-destructive life, there is no Time like Now to take the first step onto a path toward a Mindful life, a healthier life, a good life.

All in all, Life is about "Being" and becoming a better "You," living a better Life, a happier Life. Being a better "You"; put down the book and call someone just to say you were thinking about them, that you called just to chat or to say, "I love you." Visit with someone, if only for a few moments; give someone a big HUG; kiss someone in the forehead; offer to do a favor and you will have Loved someone. Whatever you choose to do, do it "Now." Let go of yourself and Love more often and always remain mindful that the word "Love" is a verb and that the word "Is" expresses Presence in a Living Moment best lived in the Present Positive Tense. So, love "Now"; it *is* the only Time you can; it may be the last Time you can. It's "Now" O'clock: Time to make a difference; Time to choose. As they say, and it is true, "There is no Time like the Present."

Keep in mind that life is about people being here for one another and that Love, Compassion, Forgiveness, and Happiness are not devices of Modernity. These are attributes of our own natural *Humanness*.

It's Life. It's Life-Time as it is and always will be, Now O'clock, Time to "Be" mindful and in control; Time to slow down and *taste* Life one *sip* at a time.

NOW

*And it dawned upon me that there is but one Life,
The Life of the living, the Life of the NOW,
And that soon, "Now" will come to pass,
Memories of yesterday, dreams of tomorrow, today,
As Life, "is" "NOW."
But the NOWs come and then they pass,
As Life shifts from Time to Time, from NOW to NOW,
Still, always in the NOW.
For there is no Life in the Past and no Life in the Future,
No Life in Memories, no Life in Dreams,
Just Life NOW, to Reminisce or to Hope,
A Life that "was," a Life that "is," a Life that is "to be."
A Life that began some NOW ago with so many Dreams,
With so little Memory,
And I know that as I shift with Time and into the winter of my
Life, Snowflakes will settle in my Hair,
The memories will fill my Mind. The dreams will be Few.
So few they may very well be only about NOWs long past.
Being Mindful, I better do it NOW.*

www.ingramcontent.com/pod-product-compliance
Lightning Source LLC
Chambersburg PA
CBHW051756040426
42446CB00007B/399